HIDDEN WOMEN

Mines, Temples & Parklands in Celtic Europe

HIDDEN WOMEN

Mines, Temples & Parklands in Celtic Europe

Jacqueline Widmar Stewart

ISBN: **979-8-8831216-8-4**

LEXICUS PRESS © 2024
PALO ALTO, CALIFORNIA
LEXICUSPRESS.COM
HIDDENWOMENBOOKS.COM

THE COMPLETE HIDDEN WOMEN SERIES:

> *A HISTORY OF EUROPE, CELTS & FREEDOM*
> *CELTIC BURGUNDY & EUROPE*
> *FRANKISH SPLENDOR & VALOR IN CELTIC EUROPE*
> *CHARLEMAGNE'S CELTIC DOMAIN*
> *LEGACIES FROM A FREE CELTIC EUROPE*
> *MINES, TEMPLES & PARKLANDS IN CELTIC EUROPE*

GRAPHIC DESIGN: REMY STEINER
EDITOR: BLAIR W. STEWART
PHOTOGRAPHY: JACQUELINE WIDMAR STEWART

GREAT THANKS TO SUZANNE ROTH & ELENA DANIELSON

SPECIAL RECOGNITION TO *DE RE METALLICA* BY GREOGIUS AGRICOLA
TRANSLATED BY LOU HENRY & HERBERT HOOVER

HIDDEN WOMEN

Mines, Temples & Parklands in Celtic Europe

the HIDDEN WOMEN *series*

Lady and the Unicorn Tapestry, Museum of the Middle Ages, Paris,

Detail golden winged horse. Chatillon-sur-Seine, France

Coin Iron Age, Celtic

AUTHOR'S NOTE

What first turned our attention to Celtic Europe? Gold. What did the Celts have that Julius Caesar wanted? Gold. Why would Russia attack Ukraine? Maybe because one of the largest gold mines in the world is located in Ukraine.

In this last volume in the HIDDEN WOMEN series, we end where we started, with the tale of gold and attackers who try to steal it. But gold is only part of the story. The knowledge and skills necessary to extract and process metals and minerals factors in, and so does the mining culture that protects miners and lands while extracting the treasures.

These are some of the inquiries in this book. If they resonate with you, please take the torch and run with it. We have worlds to uncover.

Suessiones coin. Belgic tribe conquered by Caesar

AN ODE TO NATURE'S BOUNTY

The annals of civilization
are etched in the walls of the mines.
Even old Stone Agers
Loved gold for its marvelous shine.

Then Roman exploitations
Diverted the powerful streams.
They took down entire mountains,
And seized gold by whatever means.

Rome was thrown out of Europe;
Earth's scars began to heal.
Then imperialism came back
To rampage with greater zeal.

The Industrial Revolution
Doubled down on imperial times.
Humans meant nothing –
Despots pinched every dime.

Let's bring back Celtic ideals –
The future is on the line.
A good place to start –
Honor Nature and her mines.

Golden hat. Speyer, Germany

Annaberg secular mining altar

INTRODUCTION

Women and Miners – doubly under fire.
Both possess capacity to yield
Riches beyond compare.

What does the history of mining have to do with women? Even the record written in the days of feudal Europe shows that women have been as involved in mining as they have in other aspects of early European life. Some mines are even named after women, as in Sainte-Marie-aux-Mines and the Marie-Louise mines. Tributes to women also frequently occur as plaques and imagery in the halls of mining towns.

Imagery of women has been found in the earliest known mines; gold jewelry and gemstones from those mines have been uncovered in women's graves. Medieval depictions show women working in mines, in what are likely reflections of ancient customs.

A TRIBUTE TO FRENCH FRIENDS

*This photo gallery
of a Neolithic-Merovingian-Parisian treasure
is dedicated to the Marty and Schilis families
who have led us into Celtic realms
with grace, knowledge and delights.*

*St. Maur des Fossées and Créteil
sit across from each other
on a carefully sculpted loop
in the Marne River,
augmented by races that drive the mills.*

*The lake at Créteil fills a former quarry.
The vicinity is rich in parklands.
Abbey gardens, round Merovingian towers,
Exquisite archways and stone walls
Sing the songs of Celts.*

**ST. MAUR DES FOSSÉES
SKETCH**

(📖) TOUR RABELAIS

Fleuron du patrimoine saint-maurien, l'abbaye de Saint-Maur-des-Fossés s'inscrit parmi les plus anciennes et les plus prestigieuses fondations monastiques de France.

Elle connut, de l'époque mérovingienne à sa démolition ordonnée en 1750, une histoire mouvementée représentée aujourd'hui encore par de nobles vestiges.

Les informations textuelles et cartographiques (📖) jalonnant le parc, aident à mieux connaître ce site, classé au titre des monuments historiques en 1988.

Le parc de l'Abbaye s'étend sur une superficie de 20 000 m². La partie située près de la tour d'enceinte dite Rabelais, a été aménagée en square traditionnel dès 1935 et accueille les enfants ; l'allée du Jeu d'Arc permet d'accéder aux lieux sacrés et de découvrir, dans un jardin créé à cet effet en 1982, l'ampleur de l'ancienne abbaye de Saint-Maur-des-Fossés.

(📖) GRILLES

(📖) MUR DU CELLIER

(📖) VILLA BOURIÈRES

(📖) GALERIE DE CLOÎTRE

(📖) CHAPELLE N.D. DES MIRACLES

(📖) PLAN

(📖) MUR DU CELLIER

Rue (📖) TOU

0 5 10   20   50

AUR-DES-FOSSÉS
L'ABBAYE

Saint-Maur

PILIER DE L'ÉGLISE ABBATIALE

DE L'ÉGLISE ABBATIALE

L'ABBAYE DE
ST-MAUR-DES-FOSSÉS

GRILLES

CHAPELLE NOTRE-DAME
DES MIRACLES

GALERIE DE CLÔITRE

ST. MAUR DES FOSSÉES
ABBEY MAP

ST. MAUR DES FOSSÉES
ABBEY GARDENS

ST. MAUR DES FOSSÉES
ABBEY

ST. MAUR DES FOSSÉES
SHADES OF MEROVINGIANS

ST. MAUR DES FOSSÉES
ARCHWAY

ST. MAUR DES FOSSÉES
RACES IN THE MARNE

ST. MAUR DES FOSSÉES
HEDGES & TREES

ARTIST:
JULES JACQUES LABATUT

ST. MAUR DES FOSSÉES
STATUE CARRYING
WOUNDED WOMAN

TABLE OF CONTENTS

I. OLD MINING CULTURE IN NEOLITHIC
   & CELTIC EUROPE   52

   Mountains rich in resources
   drew mines, abbeys, hot
   springs resorts and fest
   halls. Ancient mining
   cultures of Michelsberg and
   Magdalensberg spread ancient
   technology and festivity. Gold
   still draws predatory attacks

   PHOTO GALLERY   121
   Selections from *DE RE METALLICA*

II. THE PERILS OF IMPERIAL EUROPE   142

    When Gram escaped at the turn
    of the 20th century empires
    exploited natural resources
    and expended human lives

with reckless abandon. The Ruhr
Valley was plunged from a verdant
fertile valley into a toxic inferno. The
imperial church state had burned
countless thousands of women at
the stake and christianity was still
the state religion, still intolerantly
exclusive

III. OLD WORLD WAYS THAT SUSTAINED
IMMIGRANTS IN NEW WORLD MISERIES

The immigrant grandparents
left a massive proliferation of
deadly rhineland coal mines
to the explosive, black-lung
inducing ones of southern
Illinois. Having to send their
children away just out of
elementary school for their own
safety, miners struggled to gain
humane working conditions and
kept their old mining
traditions alive

IV. TWELVE CURRENT TRIBUTES TO THE
OLD CULTURE THAT WOULD HEARTEN
OUR ANCESTORS

The European Union and UNESCO
are returning enlightment to the
European voyage. They make it
possible to study public treasures
in wondrous park settings, to

enjoy gracious local hospitality,
and to expand enrichment-filled
travel

TIMELINE

THE STONE AGE

FROM CA. 3,400,000 TO 4000 B.C.E.

A broad prehistoric period during which stone was widely used to make stone tools with an edge, a point, or a percussion surface. The period lasted for roughly 3.4 million years and ended between 4,000 B.C.E and 2,000 B.C.E, with the advent of metalworking.

THE EARLY IRON AGE

FROM CA. 1200 TO 550 B.C.E.

The final epoch of the three prehistorical Metal Ages, after the Copper and Bronze Ages.

THE ROMAN EMPIRE

FROM THE 1ST CENTURY B.C.E. TO CA 476 C.E.

Julius Caesar carried out concerted Roman attacks against Europe that began in the first century B.C.E. By the 3rd century, Romans were annexing Gallic lands in southern France, seizing the lands and subjugating the Galls as Roman property. Under the leadership of Franks and Burgundians, Celtic families banded together and ousted the emperor Constantine from Rome's headquarters in Trier in ca. 476. The Roman Catholic Church then established a new capital in Byzantium, changed the name to Constantinople (now Istanbul), and carried out campaigns of terror against Eastern Europe and Africa for the following approximately 1000 year.s

THE REALM OF FRANCIA

FROM 5TH CENTURY TO CHRISTIANIZATION

Led by male and female Franks and Burgundians after the fall
of Rome in ca. 476, first by the Merovingians and then the
Carolingians, the bounds of the free Celtic world of Francia
fluctuated. A system of abbeys, castles and hot spring resorts
connected all of Europe and the British Isles; trade flourished. Under
Charlemagne, the systems of mines, abbeys, castles and hot springs
health resorts exploded in number. Typically located near natural
resource deposits, the abbeys served as centers of education and
production for mines as well as wines and spirits. Both castles and
abbeys were fortified to fend off attackers; foods and wines were
developed to sustain defenders under sieges that sometimes lasted
for years.

THE HAPSBURG EMPIRE

FROM THE 13TH CENTURY UNTIL ITS DISBANDING IN 1918

The dictatorial male supremacist church state from Rome
overtook free Celtic duchies, commandeered the nomenclature
and subjugated free Eastern Europe. As set out by the victors,
the conventional history remains highly suspect, as is true for all
accounts rendered under the Christian church state.

THE SPANISH EMPIRE

FROM CA 1492 TO THE 20TH CENTURY

called a colonial empire and sometimes referred to as the
Hispanic Monarchy or the Catholic Monarchy based in Spain.
The "discovery" of the Americas well may have been conquerors
chasing their prey across the seas to the "new world," once ships
became ocean-faring.

THE CHRISTIANIZATION OF EUROPE

FROM CA 380 TO PRESENT

The Roman Empire officially adopted Christianity in 380 C.E. During the Early Middle Ages, most of Europe was subject to Christianization, including the Rhineland Massacres of 1096 in France and Germany against Jewish families, the Albigensian Crusade against southern France, 1209 – 1229 and the Baltic Crusades against the Lithuanians, Estonians, Finns and Slavs in the 1400s. This colonization was carried out through attacks by armed warrior-monks who killed and subjugated Europeans under the banner of the Roman Catholic religion. Chrisianity converted Celtic secular domains into religious ones, privatized public property, made women the property of men, discriminated against women and non-Christians, attempted to erase the role of women, Celts and Jews in Europe's past, and changed the accepted norm of social attitudes and behavior to intolerance and exclusivity.

HIDDEN WOMEN

Mines, Temples & Parklands in Celtic Europe

HALLEIN
MOUNTAINS

ERZGEBERGE
OUT OF FREIBERG

EIFEL
MOUNTAINS

PYRENEES
MOUNTAINS

THE ANCIENT MINING CULTURE IN NEOLITHIC & CELTIC EUROPE

The Stone Age, The Iron Age & Middle Ages

Die Radeberger Exportbierbrauerei Aktiengesellschaft Radeberg widmet Herrn Georg Hillig, Gottleuba "Gasthof zum Kronprinz" aus Anlass einer 25 jährigen, für beide Teile angenehmen Geschäftsverbindung, dieses GEDENKBLATT

Dresden, am 19. Februar 1935

Bad Gottleuba

THE TREASURE VAULTS OF TIME

Gleaming like the precious resources they hold,
Europe's soaring mountains seem to radiate
the spirit of early mining towns.

Mines mirror a rich proud past of prizing and extracting
precious resources from the earth.
The towns that sprouted near mining camps
reflect a shared prosperity and exuberance
that transcends the ages.

The history of mining evokes a past like hidden women.
It hasn't always been this way for miners either,
and it doesn't need to be this way now

Bad Gottleuba

 curious starting point, but I'll commence on a note of food and drink for three reasons. It's because my grandmother survived on her cooking and baking, because wine-making and food have been such an integral part of our family history and because the ancient mining sites we've visited in Europe have astonished us with their gracious hospitality and charm.

I credit my maternal grandmother's ability to make something sumptuous from the most basic of ingredients as one of the main reasons I'm here today. My grandmother could start with some dry cream of wheat in a bare pan and end up with a toasted, savory porridge that everyone clamored to have. Both she and my mother possessed an encyclopedic knowledge of seasonings, herbs and spices, as well as of gardening itself.

Before we talk about southern Illinois where all of my grandparents spent times in mining camps, though, I'd like to give a cursory overview of some of the ancient European mines. We haven't been to every one of them, but thanks to Google, Wikipedia and Mindat, I have patched together a rough sketch of this oft-disparaged line of work. I find the care and skill evident in early mining to be awe-inspiring and I hope you will too.

There is another aspect that this inquiry into mining has exposed. On our recent visits to early mining towns and museums in what is now Spain and France, we have seen how these areas were so severely impacted by the imperial Roman Conquest that the scars are still visible. My goal here is to prompt further attention to this topic, not only relating to Rome but to subsequent invaders as well.

I will begin with samples of the numerous mines from the Stone Age and move from there to Iron Age and Roman times to see what was mined and how people were mining - all as a back-drop to the scene my grandparents encountered in the old and new worlds.

One quick word about the title. Mines have been key for me in identifying the ancient reverence for the natural world, because I know my own family's devotion to nature and I see that devotion repeatedly expressed in the Celtic world. Temples are a form of tribute to natural wonders, in the way that statuary honors heroes. Parklands belong to the old concepts of public domain, along with halls, abbeys and castles. Here's a note of interest. Ancient Hebrew texts apparently refer not to temples, a word not yet coined at the time, but to a "sanctuary", "palace" or "hall".

Eifel Mountains

THE STONE AGE

A Neolithic Michelsberg Mining Culture

The Neolithic or New Stone Age is an archaeological period, the final division of the Stone Age in Europe, Asia and Africa. It saw the Neolithic Revolution, a wide-ranging set of developments that appear to have arisen independently in several parts of the world. Start date: 10,000 B.C.E. The fifth millennium. The emergence of cultural diversity in central European prehistory.

Map showing the extent of the Michelsberg culture and its relation with surrounding areas.[4]

Aachen, germany. Mural from Granus Hotel

Flint in Aachen and Spiennes

Hot sulfur springs may have first attracted people to Aachen, the early settlement that is situated between Brussels and Cologne and has been inhabited for at least 5000 years. The discovery of flint later was a natural to ancient settlers because it occurred above-ground and breaks easily into big pieces. The area is rich in resources - 206 minerals are currently associated with Aachen.

Axes and blades don't normally come to my mind with flint. Growing up, my cousins in Illinois collected flint arrowheads from the fields, the size that Native Americans

used for arrows. An axe blade puts the flint at Aachen into a whole different category.

Three hills in this region were mined for flint as far back as 3000 B.C.E. but stone tools have been made of flint for the past three million years. Flint is one of the primary materials that defines the Stone Age, especially because it allowed people living in caves to tunnel further into the mountain. In mineral-rich areas, endless delights awaited them.

The neolithic Michelsberg mining culture has been associated with this area that encompassed the Rhineland, Belgium and Luxembourg. The Michelsberg – Michel hill - itself is located near Heidelberg. "Berg" may be short for

Bergwerke, or mines, berg meaning "hill." But, if you ignore the spelling, the sound of Michel sounds like the Slovenian word miši, which means mice. In some languages, the letter "l" is sometimes added as a diminutive suffix. So, Michelsberg might mean "little mouse hill" for all the underground mining and tunnelling that went on there. This doesn't sound quite so farfetched if you consider that in Paris, Montsouris means "mouse hill" for a mount that was mined for limestone.

Aachen chapel

Aachen. Image of Charlemagne in thermal baths

Here's another thought about names. Aachen is also known as Aix-la-Chapelle. Aix or Ax seems to have been favored by Celts to mean X or crossroads – like Aix-les-Bains, Aix-en-Provence, Dax (d'Ax), Ax-les-Thermes.

In the 9th century, Charlemagne chose Aachen as his final resting place.

Monschau panoramic view

UNESCO is protecting the neolithic mines at Spiennes as a heritage site. Neolithic mining of flint marked a seminal stage of human technological and cultural progress. Mons in Belgium may be the largest and earliest concentration of ancient mines in northwest Europe. Two chalk plateaus cover a network of galleries that riddle the earth below.

The underground tunnels are linked to the surface by vertical shafts that were dug by Neolithic people thousands of years ago and remained in operation for multiple centuries. The mines portray the advancement of mining techniques known and developed by Europe's prehistoric residents. They display a wide range of ancient mining techniques as well as being associated with a habitat that has been remarkably unspoiled by subsequent inhabitants.

Here's a description of the technique employed some 4000 years ago: *The standardization of production bears witness to*

the highly skilled craftsmanship of the stone-cutters of Spiennes. The vestiges of a fortified camp have also been discovered at the site comprising two irregular concentric pits Neolithic populations could pass below levels made up of large blocks of flint (up to 2m in length) that they extracted using a particular technique called 'striking' (freeing from below with support of a central chalk wall, shoring up the block, removal of the wall, removal of props and lowering of the block).[5]

Stone-working ateliers were also part of the mining operations here, as evidenced by the remaining flint fragments at Camp à Cayaux, or Stone Field. The blades made here were used for axes for tree-cutting and long blades for tools.

The archaeological artefacts discovered at this site are characteristic of the Michelsberg culture associated with mining. Note also that the prior name for Monschau was Montjoie, or Mountain of Joy.[6]

Gava terrain evinces mining

Variscite in Spain

Neolithic mines, in Gavá, southwest of Barcelona date back some 5000 years ago to the 4th millennium before the Common Era. All the way back in the Stone Age Europe's inhabitants tunneled four levels down into the earth to mine a pale blue-green gemstone known as variscite. Variscite beads and necklaces from grave finds are displayed in archeological museums in both Barcelona and Madrid, and those graves were typically women's.

Gavá, Spain, variscite vein in Stone Age mine

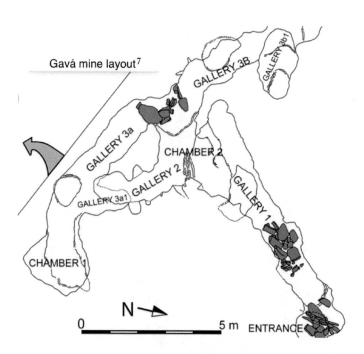

Gavá mine layout[7]

GALLERY 3B

GALLERY 3b1

GALLERY 3a

CHAMBER 2

GALLERY 3a1

GALLERY 2

GALLERY 1

CHAMBER 1

N →

0   5 m   ENTRANCE

Gavá, Spain, varascite mine location. Map by Mindat

Variscite in grave find

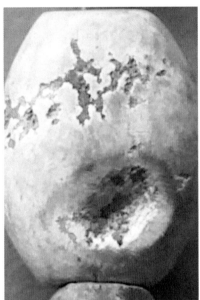
Variscite bead

Venus of Gavà

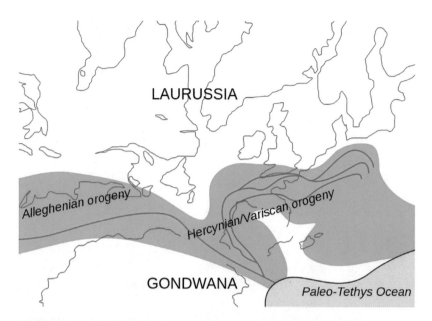

Variscan orogeny. In geologic terms, here are the Hercynian-Alleghenian mountain belts in the middle of the Carboniferous period. Present day coastlines are shown in grey. An orogeny, or mountain-building, is the result of collision between two landmasses

Here's a technical description of the process by which this beautiful mineral was created: *The Variscan or Hercynian orogeny was a mountain-building event caused by Late Paleozoic continental collision between Euramerica (Laurussia) and Gondwana to form the supercontinent of Pangaea, some 200 million years ago.* This collision resulted in the creation of the gemstone variscite that can be found in Spain.

Variscite itself is named for Variscia, the historical name of the Vogtland, in Germany. So, it appears that variscite was mined in the Neolithic era in what is now Spain, but also in the former Varisia in the Ore Mountains that straddle the area now shared by Germany and the Czech lands.

Turning to the physical aspects of the Spanish mine, the complex layering of galleries and chambers from the Stone Age obviously required substantial engineering knowledge. Also worthy of note is that the extraction of minerals and metals went hand in hand with processing, which was also more advanced than usual notions of Stone Age activities bring to mind. Traces of metallurgy workshops dating back to neolithic times were found right at the mining site.

Gavá neolithic mines

Neolithic mining site at Gavà, 4th millennium B.C.E (Kunst 2001)

Gavá, photo by Museu de Ciències Naturals de Barcelona

That's the significance of variscite and how it formed near Barcelona. Let's step back and look at the context. What were the circumstances of people living in the Stone Age who began tunneling into the mountain to secure this desirable stone?

A glance at the map shows considerable open space in the hilly terrain of the Gava-Barcelona area, with each end of crescent-shaped Gava capped by green. The naturally contoured and rugged wilderness that is preserved as public lands could suggest that open access has been a tradition there for a long time, perhaps as long as human habitation.

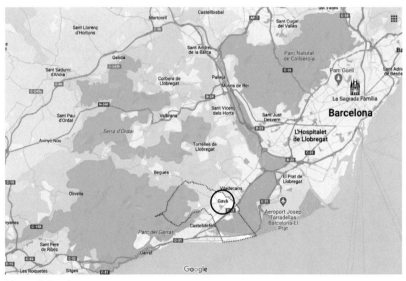

Map of Gavá

The city of Barcelona is wedged between two rivers and flanked by the sea. The 4th side of its natural buffer system comes from the north, where the majestic Pyrennées stretch across the narrow neck that connects Spain with the rest of Europe. These borders of rivers, sea and mountain serve as natural defensive protections surrounding the city.

THE SALT OF THE EARTH – MINED IN EUROPE FOR 7000 YEARS

Salt in Hallein and Wieliczka

Another type of mining that occurred in the neolithic era around 4000 B.C.E revolves around the discovery that salt could be used to preserve food. By the 6th century B.C.E., Celts were tunnelling some 3 miles into Salzburg's Dürrnberg mountain to mine vast stores of salt it held deep inside. Archeological finds in that area, now in northern Austria, indicate a far-reaching Celtic trade in gold, coral and amber as well.[8]

Hallein

Hallein salt mine

The Salzburg and Salzkammergut areas are located close together in the eastern Alps and make up the richest salt deposits in Middle Europe. The mines at Hallstatt, Hallein-Durrnberg and Bad Reichenhall cluster together, while Bad Aussee lies further east.

During World War II Hallein was a work camp annex to Dachau concentration camp, and after the war served as a permanent Displaced Persons camp -called Beth Israel. In 1948 Hallein became the Austrian hub for Jewish emigrants to the United States and Canada.

Hallein in the Salzkammergut

Wieliczka salt mine gallery. Wikipedia photo

Wieliczka salt mine interior

Since neolithic times salt has been mined in Wieliczka
near Kraków, now southern Poland. Until it closed in 1996,
Wieliczka was one of the world's oldest operating salt mines. Now
an official Polish Historic Monument (Pomnik Historii) and
a UNESCO World Heritage Site, its features that are open to
the public include shafts and labyrinths, displays of historic salt-
mining technology, and an underground lake.[9]

Bad Gottleuba-Berggiesshübel. Hot springs resort town near Marie Louise Stolln mines

Early Tin & Silver in the Ore Mountains

As early as 3000 B.C.EE, Europe's inhabitants were making bronze from tin and copper. By this time, both in the Balkans and the Middle East, tin by itself already was well-known and used. Tin was traded north to the Baltic Sea and south to the Mediterranean, following the old Amber Road.

The Karlovy Vary District in the Ore Mountains contains combinations of hot springs resorts and mining towns.

Jáchymov, for example, has been producing silver for thousands of years and has gained protection as a UNESCO World Heritage Site. Jáchymov was also the site of the first radium mine in the world.[10]

Karlovy Vary remained a highly desirable town in the age of Charlemagne, not only for hot springs, but obviously also because of the mineral rich Ore Mountains. Gracious esplanades with fountains of mineral springs, parks, architectural gems and inviting cafés line the river banks.

Now the Ore Mountains are a UNESCO Heritage Site. The region includes many well-preserved relics from derelict mines, including the mines themselves, mine shafts, smelters, and hammer mills. The World Heritage Site comprises 22 mining sites and monuments, 17 in Germany and 5 in the Czech Republic.

Jáchymov crest

Panorama view of the Karlovy Vary town, in 1715. Mindat.org

Karlovy Vary, or Carlsbad

At first impression, the areas of Karlovy Vary appear to be divided into districts. The green hills lie to the left, with the residential area following the river. It looks as though mined areas may have been replanted with trees. The fields are grouped to the right of the town.

	21. Der Thurm,
	22. Die Apotheke,
	23. Die Kayserl. Mauth
	24. Das Mühl Bad.
	25. Schlakenwalder Ther
	26. Das Schiehaus

Karlovy Vary pavillon

Jáchymov

Formerly known as Joachimsthal, Jacymov became known for silver in the 15th century and minted the silver coins Joachimsthalers, or thalers. Later a black substance brought renewed attention to the area when it was identified as radium, isolated by Marie Curie.

The Svornost mine claims to be the oldest mine still in use in Europe, in operation since 1525. For a long time it was the only place where radium was mined and the world's leading source of radium.

Jachymov Agricola spa. Wikipedia photo

Goslar Lohmühle

Clausthal

Rammelsberg, a Hartz Mountain mine from the Bronze Age

Zinc, copper, gold and silver count among the riches of Rammelsberg, a mine in the Hartz mountains. Ore mining was going on here in the Bronze Age, with the "old bed" or "old orebody" that erosion had exposed at the surface. The mining museum became a UNESCO World Heritage project

Goslar and Rammelsberg, 1574 depiction, Matz Sincken

along with Goslar's Old Town. In 2010 this World Heritage Site was expanded to include the Walkenried Abbey and the historic Samson Pit. The Rammelsberg Museum and Visitor Mine is an anchor point on the European Route of Industrial Heritage (ERIH)[11]

The hot springs resort town of Bad Harzburg lies a short 8 miles from Goslar. The proximity of baths to mining town adds further evidence of its Celtic roots.

Wales stone house, slate roof

Thuringa, near Celle, Frankenau and Frankenbert

Slate in Thuringa, slate in Wales

The slate in Thuringia, now eastern Germany, links to the Michelsberg neolithic culture from the Rhineland. Later, under Charlemagne in the 9th century, Thuringa is said to have flourished with mines, abbeys and castles.

The slate in Wales has been mined for over 1800 years, and dates back about 500 million years. Europe shares many mineral deposit formations with the British Isles.

THE IRON AGE

Magdalena and mining

Here I want to touch briefly on the name Magdalena and mines. Apparently the Magdalena neolithic mining culture spread tools and knowledge broadly in Europe.

Magdalena and its many variations may stem from the ancient site of Magdala on the Sea of Galilee. The name Magdalena has been attached to places all over Europe; it is associated with "berg" in German-speaking countries and "gora" in Slavic speaking ones, as in Magdalensberg, Magdalenska gora.

Donzenac, a former slate mining town

Donzenac, Pans de Travassac. Pull-apart slate mountains

Michelsberg and Magdalensberg both appear to reach back to the Stone Age mining traditions. Those who settled in the Périgord in the Magdalenian era likely came from the Middle East, bringing the name from the ancient site of Magdala. Michel and Magdalena – as well as iterations such as Michael, Majda – both had European roots millennia before Christianity was brought to Europe. Both connect with mining through pre-Christian Iron Age settlements, but also in their naming.

The Berg in both names is likely short for Bergwerke - which means mines - and both areas are rich in natural resources. In both areas the stone occurs in easy, ready-to-use form. The Michelsberg area is rich in flint; la Madeleine in slate. Both flint and slate break in sheets, with no tools or tunnelling required, and perfect for Stone Age useage.

Paris. La Madeleine

Paris. La Madeleine. Note serpent at her foot

Bad Waltersdort. Magdalena   **Lemburg. Magdalena**

The Magdalenian culture derives from the geologic era just after the last Ice Age about 20,000 years ago and is known for its decorative arts and domestication of small animals.

In prehistory before the Roman invasions, Magdalensberg near Maria Saal, Austria, was said to be the capital of Celtic Noricum. Eight of 13 families associated with Noricum have apparently been identified by the excavations on the Magdalensberg: Ambidraven, Ambilines, Ambitious, Helvetian ("Elveti"), Laianken, Noriker, Saevaten and Uperaken.[13]

Noricum is rich in gold and iron ore, and is credited with the invention of the ploughshare, horticultural and technological skills. Noricum is known especially for Noric steel sword, as memorialized by Ovid: "harder than iron which Noric fire tempers".[14]

Magdalensberg, mining village and Capital of Noricum, fell to Roman invaders

Magdalensberg, hilltop fort

When Rome invaded, some Celts apparently fled Noricum to settle in the Po Valley and Venice.[15] Areas still bearing the name Magdalena typically have been mined since before the Roman invasion and empire. Some, like St. Magdalena just east of Seville, in the south of Spain, evince succumbing to Christian conquest by having "Saint" in front of their name. For millennia now, these Sierra Morena mountains have been mined for copper, gold and silver.

The Roman Empire left a huge mark on European mining. From what we've seen, Roman and Christian behavior for the past 2000+ years is consistent with their teachings. The idea that

Magdalensberg ancient gold mines near Maria Saal

La Madeleine cave interior in the Périgord

everyone who wasn't a Roman citizen was a barbarian – that is emblematic of Christian teachings of exclusivity and intolerance. Non-Christians and their lands thus become the enemy to be vanquished in every way possible. Mines exhibit these 2000-year-old attitudes in a raw and poignant way. Romans applied different laws to different segments of the populations, and Christianity has continued that Roman practice.

Please see the endnote for more information about Magdalena in the new world.[16]

The 4th book of the Hidden Women series Charlemagne's Celtic Domain addresses the proliferation of slate mines under Charlemagne. The 5th book Legacies from a Free Celtic Europe talks about La Madeleine in France's Périgord and how the migrants found shelter in the caves there after the end of the last Ice Age, in the era of the Stone Age. Now I'd like to revisit La Madeleine regarding the mining of slate in the Stone Age.

The Stone Age is characterized for people of that era living in caves and making tools of stone. The caves that sit above a loop in a river high on a rock face offered an ideal perch for keeping families safe and sheltered. Tying a stone to a stick of wood, Stone Age inhabitants of La Madeleine made a hammer to customize the dwelling by carving out more rooms from the immense rock outcropping.

The biggest surprises in the cave at la Madeleine were the beauty of the spaces and the fact that people living millennia ago had a bakery in the cave.

A bakery in the Stone Age – how could that happen? Stones are in abundant supply so simply by stacking some up and placing some slate across the top and against the opening - voilà. Slate is plentiful in the Périgord and people have known how to build a fire for a million years, so those were not issues.

How do you move food in and out of that oven in the Stone Age? Here again, slate is the answer - the perfect ancient baking sheet.

Its location in the subterranean caves of La Madeleline kept this Stone Age village from being destroyed in the Ice Age. Glaciation sheered off much of the physical record of past habitations. These caves visible today used to be much deeper underground than they now are.

Like Gavá, Madeleine was well-situated in terms of natural protections. Its vantage point high on a high, steep cliff overlooking a loop in the river kept it hidden from view. The region is full of caves, so tunnelling naturally followed.

La Madeleline, a path along the cliff

Slate easily obtained in the region likely aided these cave dwellers in both building and baking. Once cave dwellers began building free-standing structures, it would not take long to figure out that the sheets of slate could be overlapped to form a roof.

Cabanes du Breuil in the Perigord

Slate roofed houses in the Périgord now

Nouvelle-Aquitaine

Let's spend a minute on the broader context. The Périgord sits just east of Bordeaux, an ancient port, winemaking center, and also known for Celtic Druids, famous for teaching and negotiating skills.It makes sense that the area has been inhabited since the Stone Age. The wealth of resources in the area includes the thermal baths at Dax which lies not far to the south, a nice seasonal alternative to the caves.

The Nouvelle-Aquitaine area is rich in minerals, including aggregates, barite, coal, gold, granite, gypsum, lead, limestone, silver, slate, tin, tungsten, uranium and zinc.

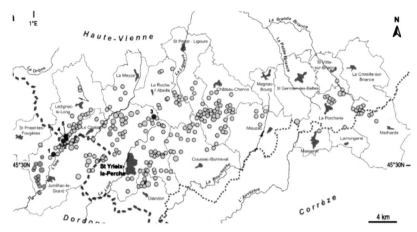

Map of gold mines in the Périgord[17]

Bordeaux – Limoges – Toulouse: all 3 cities seem to link arms around the Perigord. Each was the capital city for an ancient Celtic family. Bordeaux – known as Burdigala was the capital of the Bituriges Vivisci family; Limoges was the capital of the Lemovices family; Toulouse may have been the capital for the Volcae family, although it also had historic ties with the Franks and renown Frankish-Celtic leader Charlemagne. Bordeaux is linked to Toulouse by the Garonne River; Limoges is the capital of the Limousin region, graced with ancient Celtic gold mines.

By the Iron Age La Tène period around 750 years B.C.E. west central Gaul, as the Limousin region was then known, inhabitants had developed more ways to extract the natural bounty in their region. More than 250 prehistoric gold mining sites - including over 1100 opencast individual mines operated by the Celtic tribe known as Lemovices - were identified in Limousin in the Périgord, now in the southeastern part of Nouvelle Aquitaine.

The Lemovici family there followed hydrothermal veins of gold deep into the earth. As they tunneled along veins they propped up their tunnels with pillars, and some of those pillars have been found, still in their original placement, almost 3000 years later.

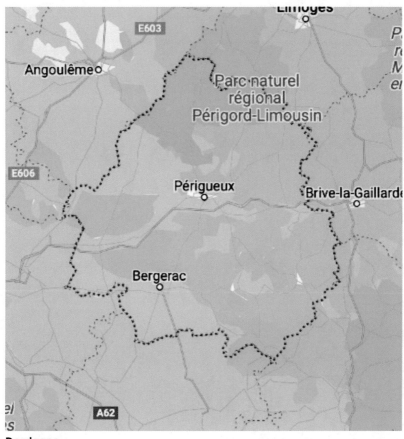

Dordogne

Early Celtic mining also appears to have comprised processing right on site. Evidence of roasting hearths, crushing tables, millstones, ore washing tables and crucibles shows the extent of Iron Age gold mining capabilities.

Iron in the Iron Age — From Fontenay Abbey to Bohinj

The forge, the smithy, the hearth. These were everywhere that iron ore could be easily obtained, from the Ore Mountains to the Alpine summits of Slovenia's Bohinj.

Fontenay forge

At the edge of the forest where wood was a step away, charcoal was made for the smelting process in the mounds made by stacking the wood carefully in circles – close to where the wood is. Then there's the smelting, the creation of the iron bloom, done in furnaces close to where the ore is. The initial forging can be done anywhere that you want to take the bloom. You end up with billets of iron that can be carried around to other places and worked there. A billet is described as a solid semi-finished round or square product that has been hot worked by forging, rolling or extrusion. An iron or steel billet has a minimum width or thickness of 1 1/2 in. and the cross-sectional area varies from 2 1/4 to 36 sq.[18]

Fontenay Abbey cloister

The ancient iron production in Bohinj was proven mostly by slag heaps, according to research by Ivo Janez Cundrič. Iron production had to start close to home because of the weight involved in the iron ore. Slag heaps necessarily indicate proximity to source.

The invention of iron smelting in the Iron Age marked an enormous step forward to Europe's populations. News travelled very fast – traders spread their tentacles across Europe and brought new inventions with them - but it also developed over time.[19]

HUT NEAR
BOHIN

LAKE
BOHINJ

THE CHRISTIANIZATION

The Roman Empire brought hell to Europe

Greek and Roman accounts of an afterlife seem almost light-hearted in comparison. Vastly different notions of an afterlife had imagined Elysian Fields, the River Stix, Hades, and a 3-headed dog before the invasion by Imperial Romans. Burning in hell and endless service to an angry master – those are razor-sharp in contrast to the preceding ones. Even the word itself is probably lifted from the Norse legends of Hel, either referring to a battle-axe used by Magus the Good of Norway or to the name of the entity that presides over the realm. The term "hel" is also related to hall and Valhalla – the hall of the slain - which sounds far more in keeping with secular, pre-Christian celebrations. The Celtic significance of the word "hall" itself, too, comes to bear.

When the Roman Empire swallowed Europe in the early centuries of this Common Era, the Romans changed the way mining was done. Imperial Romans also imposed inhuman conditions on miners. Here's a first-hand account by a Roman from that era.

What happens is far beyond the work of giants. The mountains are bored with corridors and galleries made by lamplight with a duration that is used to measure the shifts. For months, the miners cannot see the sunlight and many of them die inside the tunnels. This type of mine has been given the name of ruina montium. The cracks made in the entrails of the stone are so dangerous that it would be easier to find purpurine or pearls at the bottom of the sea than make scars in the rock. How dangerous we have made the Earth! Pliny the Elder.[20]

In search of Celtic gold, Romans committed atrocities to lands across the continent – from Romania to Spain. Their ferocity paralyzed their foes into submission. They worked their prey to death. Imperial conquests meant devastation not only to the habitants but to the lands.

Northern Europe was neither Roman nor Christian homeland. As such, it was there to be invaded and exploited. Attackers obliterated whole mountains that held valuable resources. Hydraulic mining methods turned alps into plains.

Evidence suggests that Jews had been active participants in mining in Iron Age, pre-Christian Europe, but that under Christian rule they were denied ownership. Explicit from official writings and actions, the Christian Church State regarded both Jews and women as enemies of the state and punishable by brutal heresy laws that were in place in Europe for 1400 years. Ostensibly these laws gave church state officials the pretense of legal underpinnings for their oppressive actions against women and Jews, even in the sphere of mining.

Since pre-Christian times, Judengasse – or Jewish Street – has been located right next to Goldgasse in Salzburg, Austria. Presumably goldsmith workshops would line Goldgasse. And Salzburg's rich Dürrnberg mountain contains not only salt, but also gold, coral and amber. Those memories waft over the salt city like faint strains from the deep past, though, because in the era of the imperial church state, only the crown could own mines.

Take the ancient and modern gold mines in Rosia Montana, Romania, in the Transylvanian Alps. Mining there began more than 2000 years ago and was overtaken by invaders. Through concerted efforts by the global secular community, ancient mining sites like this one are now being rehabilitated. In 2021 these mines in Romania became a World Heritage Area.

In chapter four, other examples of UNESCO World Heritage sites will be cited in conjunction with the work of the United Nations on restoration of mines.

Roman male Crusaders commandeered Celtic secular temples and branded them religious.

The woodcuts in this section are excerpted from the book *De Re Metallica*[21] and show medieval mining practices. From cutting tools and long-handled scoops to pillars that held up underground roofs, there appears to be a continuum of mining expertise that passed from generation to generation. Ancient axes and blades created new underground chambers and galleries; vines wove into baskets to carry rocks.

The 16th century book *De Re Metallica* yields medieval insights that correspond to ancient practices. These images seem to tie together Europe's mining past because the basic principles carry through consistently and definitively. The woodcuts in this book show medieval ways of working with stones and metals

Paimpont Abbey forges. Stone and slate

that harken back to what archeologists have found in Stone Age mining. These techniques would not be unfamiliar to today's miners.

Stone has been used for blades all the way back to the Stone Age. Big, sharp pieces of flint were easily available in what was Belgium-France-Germany in the Stone Age, and those in the Michelsberg culture made good use of that availability. The versatility of flint expanded from fire-starter to tree-cutter. Slate proved invaluable for its multiple uses too - from the oven to the roof - and with the same ease of extraction as flint.

De Re Metallica seems to encapsulate practices as they existed before the Christian Conquest, at a time when forges and metallurgy workshops were part of the venerated activity of mining. This is evident in abbeys where skills and implements related to mining were learned and taught. These were places open to all, where everyone could view the process and be a part of its celebration. Another connection – the word "trades," as in building trades and mining trades, suggests that these words originate from a practice of widespread sharing.

Pillared pavilions with arched doorways,
vaulted ceilings, brick furnaces, slate roofs,
dormer and hedges -
These were hallmarks of early mines and metallurgy.
The miseries came later.

Christianity conquered the temples
That secular Celts had erected;
The adoration of metals was twisted into
The terror of an angry god

Temples that marked the entry
Of flowing, healing waters
Now became the province of
An all-male cast of oppressors.

The hoods and robes the processors wore,
When working mines and procedures,
Now were worn by warrior monks
Bent on subjugation.

The dress of druids, embroidered and fine
Soon became the male-priest's clothing
Mining was wrenched from its vaunted heights,
Dumped to the bowels of the beast.

No facet was left untouched.
Every aspect was rendered subservient;
The lands, the air, the people, the mines
Savagely "Christianized."

Copper ores visible at the surface to neolithic Europeans. Dan Davis History, These Ancient Mines Transformed Prehistoric Europe www.youtube.com/watch?v=FL92iskCSZA

The high place of mining in European culture is striking throughout the entire book by Gregorius Agricola, *De Re Metallica*, written in the 16th century and translated by Lou Henry and Herbert Hoover. It is self-evident that the mining expertise displayed in the book builds on longtime experience and improvements. The quality and science in the illustrations alone are a testament to the millennia of advancements that led to this body of work.

Fontenay Abbey iron forging hearth

Take the description of tin processing in the 16th century exhibits, for instance, that occurred some 25 centuries of refinement from early Stone Age mining practices. Both the writing and the depiction of the tin smelters display the passion for metallurgy as well as the high regard given to the mining process. *Some build two furnaces against the wall just like those I have described and above them build a vaulted ceiling supported by the wall and by four pillars. Through holes in the vaulted ceiling the fumes from the furnaces ascend into a dust chamber, similar to the one described before, except that there is a window on each side and there is no door. The smelters, when they have to clear away*

the flue-dust, mount by the steps at the side of the furnaces, and climb
by ladders into the dust chamber through the apertures in the vaulted
ceilings over the furnaces. They then remove the flue-dust from
everywhere and collect it in baskets, which are passed from one to the
other and emptied. This dust chamber differs from the other described,
in the fact that the chimneys, of which it has two, are not dissimilar to
those of a house; they receive the fumes which, being unable to escape
through the upper part of the chamber, are turned back and re-ascend
and release the tin; thus the tin set free by the fire and turned to ash,
and the little tin-stones which fly up with the fumes, remain in the
dust chamber of else adhere to copper plates in the chimney.

The Middle Ages is often characterized as the Dark Ages, devoid of invention, and rife with superstition. In that vein it might be asserted that the illustrations in De Re Metallica have been embellished with pillars and arches that had no part in the dank grimness of the miners' world. I would offer the beauty of the hearth in Fontenay as evidence to the contrary.

The melding of art and function are striking in the depiction of medieval mining operations. Ornate pavilions mark spots of key mining importance – these surely are the temples. Here too the secular obviously preceded the religious, even though we've long been taught it was the other way around.

Pulgas water temple

De Re Metallica, page 44

Ancient Hebrew texts apparently refer not to temples, a word not yet coined at the time, but to "sanctuaries", "palaces" or "halls". "Hall," a staple Celtic term, refers to the old system of fest halls in the public domain that still occasionally remains in current names – like Schwäbish Hall and Hallstatt.

Mines apparently used to be part of the public domain. Quarries were located in public parks, available on the basis of need. Metallurgy was part of the mining operation. Working with precious metals occurred in vaunted places in the Celtic world, which seems to be the diametric opposite of the new world forced labor camps that coal miners like my grandparents experienced in southern Illinois as immigrants.

A current example of temples that mark places of public distinction is the California water temple. This monument celebrates the engineering feat of the Hetch-Hetchy water project that brought water to the Bay Area.

Lou Henry Hoover

Kudos to Lou Henry Hoover, shown with her geologists' pick. She and her mining engineer husband Herbert Hoover brought the 16th century book on mining De Re Metallica to the

fore. The couple later served as first couple at Stanford University, then as first couple of the United States. Their work enables us to see mining connections from Stone Age to Celtic Europe.

The woodcuts in this section are excerpted from the book *De Re Metallica* and show medieval mining practices. From cutting tools and long-handled scoops to pillars that held up underground roofs, there appears to be a continuum of mining expertise that passed from generation to generation.

These images seem to tie together Europe's mining past because the basic principles carry through consistently and definitively. The woodcuts in this book show medieval ways of working with stones and metals that harken back to what archeologists have found in Stone Age mining.

Stone was used for blades in the Stone Age. Big, sharp pieces of flint were there for the taking in the Stone Age; those in the Michelsberg culture made good use of that availability. The versatility of flint expanded from fire-starter to tree-cutter.

De Re Metallica, **page 326**

The stone slate also proved invaluable for its multiple uses - in the oven and on the roof, and with the same ease of extraction as flint.

Already in pre-Christian Europe, metallurgy melded processing with extraction. Furnaces, workshops and tools forged the way. Both men and women participated in ancient mining – and they brought along their dogs.

Pillared pavilions with arched doorways, vaulted ceilings, brick furnaces, scalloped tile roofs. These were hallmarks of the early mines.

The miseries came later.

The following selection of woodcuts from De Re Metallica have been chosen because they display the medieval traditions that likely derive from the Stone Age Michelsberg mining culture:

- the role of women working in the mine
- temples celebrating sources of natural bounty
- proximity of some mines to ships for ready transport
- use of wheels and gears and rotaries
- underground construction using pillars and arches
- Magdalenian reference to taming of wolves
- likely identification with refuge castle in public domain
- decoration of pillars and temples
- concern with health and safety of workers
- recognition of dangers and measures taken to counteract

PHOTO GALLERY
SELECTIONS FROM

De Re Metallica

A—Hearth of the furnace.   B—Chimney.   C—Common pillar.   D—Other pillars.
The partition wall is behind the common pillar and not to be seen.   E—Arches.
F—Little walls which protect the partition wall from injury by the fire.
G—Crucibles.   H—Second long wall.   I—Door.   K—Spatula.   L—The other
spatula.   M—The broom in which is inserted a stick.   N—Pestles.   O—Wooden
mallet.   P—Plate.   Q—Stones.   R—Iron rod.

A—Pot. B—Circular fire. C—Crucibles. D—Their lids. E—Lid of the pot.
F—Furnace. G—Iron rod.

A—Furnace in which the air is drawn in through holes. B—Goldsmith's forge.
C—Earthen crucibles. D—Iron pots. E—Block.

A—Shed. B—Painted signs. C—First room. D—Middle room. E—Third room. F—Two little windows in the end wall. G—Third little window in the roof. H—Well. I—Well of another kind. K—Cask. L—Pole. M—Forked sticks in which the porters rest the pole when they are tired.

A—Spring. B—Skin. C—Argonauts.

A—Furnaces. B—Forehearths. C—Their tap-holes. D—Dipping-pots. E—Pillars.
F—Dust-chamber. G—Window. H—Chimneys. I—Tub in which the coals are
washed.

A—Shaft. B—Bottom pump. C—First tank. D—Second pump. E—Second tank.
F—Third pump. G—Trough. H—The iron set in the axle. I—First pump rod.
K—Second pump rod. L—Third pump rod. M—First piston rod. N—Second
piston rod. O—Third piston rod. P—Little axles. Q—"Claws."

A—Axles. B—Levers. C—Toothed drum. D—Drum made of rundles.
E—Drum in which iron clamps are fixed.

A—WHEEL WHOSE PADDLES ARE TURNED BY THE FORCE OF THE STREAM. B—AXLE. C—DRUM OF AXLE, TO WHICH CLAMPS ARE FIXED. D—CHAIN. E—LINK. F—DIPPERS. G—BALANCE DRUM.

A—HEAD OF THE SLUICE. B—RIFFLES. C—WOODEN SCRUBBER. D—POINTED STICK.
E—DISH. F—ITS CUP-LIKE DEPRESSION. G—GROOVED DISH.

A—Tub. B—Sieve. C—Rods. D—Bench-frame.

A—Cross grooves. B—Tub set under the sluice. C—Another tub.

A—Water wheel of upper machine. B—Its pump. C—Its trough. D—Wheel of lower machine. E—Its pump. F—Race.

A, B—TWO FURNACES. C—FOREHEARTH. D—DIPPING-POTS. THE MASTER STANDS AT
THE ONE FURNACE AND DRAWS AWAY THE SLAGS WITH AN IRON FORK. E—IRON FORK.
F—WOODEN HOE WITH WHICH THE CAKES OF MELTED PYRITES ARE DRAWN OUT. G—THE
FOREHEARTH CRUCIBLE : ONE-HALF INSIDE IS TO BE SEEN OPEN IN THE OTHER FURNACE.
H—THE HALF OUTSIDE THE FURNACE. I—THE ASSISTANT PREPARES THE FOREHEARTH,
WHICH IS SEPARATED FROM THE FURNACE THAT IT MAY BE SEEN.   K—BAR. L—WOODEN
RAMMER. M—LADDER. N—LADLE.

Gold in Romania; Gold in Ukraine

Care versus recklessness. The effects of each can still be seen in the scars on the environment. Strains evident in the ancient Michelsberg mining culture continued in the Middle Ages, as seen through De Re Metallica. It's also apparent what damage invaders inflicted on the environment with their reckless disregard.

Like the gold mines of Médulas in Spain, Romania's gold mines were plundered by the Romans. Rome's invasion and occupation of Romania immeasurably enriched the Roman Empire and impoverished Romania.

Rosia Montana, Transylvania, Romania, gold mines. Map by Mindat

Roșia Montană Mining Landscape contains the most significant, extensive and technically diverse underground Roman gold mining complex currently known in the world, dating from the Roman occupation of Dacia (106-271 CE). Roșia Montană is situated in a natural amphitheatre of massifs and radiating valleys in the Metalliferous range of the Apuseni Mountains, located in the historical region of Transylvania in the central part of Romania. whc.unesco.org/en/list/1552/

Rosia Montana, Transylvania, Romania. Photo by Mindat

Ukraine. Carpathian Mountains

Gold, etc.

Khyr-Pilyaki rocky mountain, Goluboi Zaliv village, Simeiz area, Crimea, Ukraine

Gold

Saulyak gold deposit, Dilove village, Rakhivskiy ore camp, Rakhiv Raion, Zakarpattia Oblast, Ukraine

The Berehove mine is one of the largest gold mines in Ukraine and in the world. Located in the south-west of the country in Zakarpattia Oblast, the mine has estimated reserves of 14.4 million oz of gold and 144 million oz of silver. The mine also has ore reserves amounting to 300 million tonnes grading 1.5% lead and 2.1% zinc. *Wikipedia*

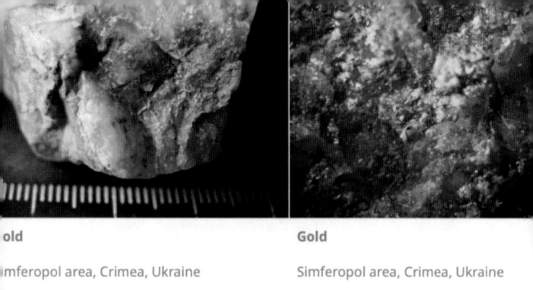

old

imferopol area, Crimea, Ukraine

Gold

Simferopol area, Crimea, Ukraine

IS UKRAINE STILL UNDER ATTACK BY AN INVADER TODAY BECAUSE OF ITS RICHES?

Ukraine. Berehova. Vidpochynkovyy Kompleks

Ukraine. Berehova mining town. Photo by Lilia Krisko

**PLEASE NOTE — THESE PHOTOS WERE TAKEN PRIOR
TO RUSSIA'S ATTACK ON UKRAINE**

Ukraine. Berehova fish pond

Ukraine. Vineyards near Berehova mining town

Berehova

THE PERILS OF IMPERIAL EUROPE

What Do Massacres Have To Do With Mining?

"WITCH HUNT"— THE MEN WHO SAY IT & THE WOMEN WHO DIE

Tens of thousands of women were killed.
In the town of Eichstatt alone
Some 400 women were tortured and died,
All burned at the stake as witches.[23]

The abbey at Eichstätt sits far down the hill
from the hall at Frauenkappelle.
Both abbey and hall still remember these women
With many distinctive images.

Not long ago the church was called down
For killing these women back then
What did they do in response?
Put up a small memorial plague.

This gesture might seem pretty nice of those men
Unless you start realizing
That they're the ones pretending that
The women were Christian martyrs.

So, when you hear "witch hunt" said by a man,
Consider pious men in the past.
And here they are now, at the ready once more
To send women to their death[24]

Eichstätt

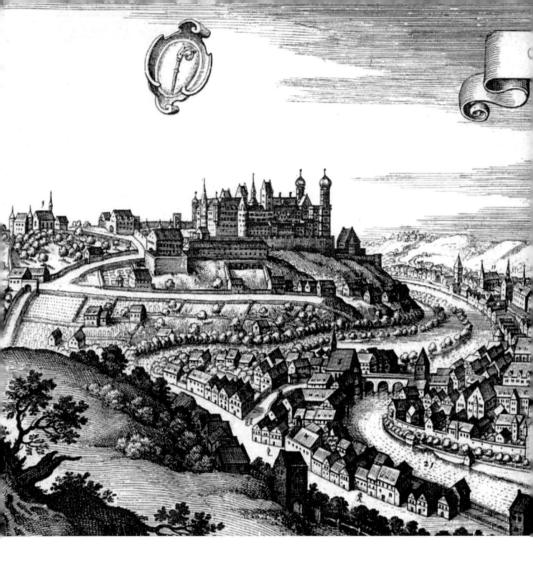

rom 1400 to 1782, it is estimated that between 40,000 and 60,000 people were accused of witchcraft and killed. Most were burned at the stake; most were women. The very heart of Europe was the area most affected, which comprises

Eichstätt or Aychstatt. Wikipedia

today's Germany, Switzerland and northeastern France. This is
the very area of Michelsberg, home of the ancient mining culture.

Eichstätt is located near Munich, Nuremberg and
Stuttgart, all with which thrived as ancient Celtic towns before
the advent of Christianity. Archaeology, mining and science
converge in Eichstätt, famous for its quarries of Soinhofen
Plattenkalk, or Jurassic limestone. Evidence shows that Celts
inhabited Eichstätt, in the *valley of the Franconian Jura*, long before
the Roman invasion.

The limestone at Eichstätt was formed in the Jurassic Era,some 200 million years ago. Ancestors knew how to use it because limestone had been mined in the Middle East since 7000 B.C.E., as evidenced by a lime mortar floor from those times. Lime is readily made by heating limestone; early civilizations used it to hold walls and floors together.

Why should empires want to attack these ancient places like Eichstätt? Mining. Celtic mining savvy is a common thread here, and women played a leading role in all facets of Celtic life, from what archeology tells us.

Ancient Celtic mining settlements such as Eichstätt appear to have been favored targets of attack. Celts developed mining expertise because they lived in areas that were richly endowed with natural resources. Mining involves science - engineering, geology, mathematics, metallurgy – not only for tunneling through mountains, but also for processing ores and minerals.

Fossils in this area evinced a world that pre-dated Christianity's 2000-year history. That posed a threat to dictators' claims of divine right of kings, their god and their story of creation.

Celts apparently thrived on scientific discovery, but the church state forbad and punished it. In the 1400 years that heresy laws were imposed on Europe by Roman law, scientific advancement was controlled by the Crown. Only official edicts issued by the Church State could be accepted as fact; dissemination of any other information – including scientific - was punishable by death under the heresy laws.

People with mining expertise seem to move around. Like the masons who helped build abbeys, castles and fest halls all over Europe, the miners would go place to place and manage projects. Judging from the mining symbols in remote graveyards, people appear to have carried mining credentials around with them in code.

Heresy, witch burnings and the paltry response by religious leaders continuing to occupy secular temples like Eichstätt – what does this have to do with my Gram's escape from Essen long after the Middle Aged frenzy around witches?

Eichstätt was on the way from Slovenia to Essen, a likely stopping point for my grandparents on their way to Essen. As mentioned, both Eichstätt and Essen belonged in the heart of the Michelsberg mining culture region. EIchstätt with its famed Jurassic limestone would have been of intense interest for a couple coming from an area like Litija, itself rich in mineral deposits. As a mining couple, my grandparents would have been warmly welcomed into this mecca mining town.

Paralleling those reasons, both Eichstätt and Essen were rich and famous mining areas that suffered at the hands of oppressors. Travelling in areas such as these at the very crossroads of ancient European passageways must have been fraught with dangers. It was important to move within the mining network along brigant-infested highways.

Christianity remains feudal to its core. Based on a masterservant, male-supremacist class system, the master owns his subservient subjects who idolize him, and women serve as men's property, their vessels.

So why would my grandparents come to Essen? One clue is that an underground railroad helped people from Eastern Europe escape through Essen, according to information in a museum near Essen. Was Essen a Christian hotbed?

Let's think about Essen itself. Essen is considered the capital of the Ruhr Valley, a place that dates all the way back to 280,000 years ago. The basis for this number comes from a flint tool called the Vogelheimer Klinge. Essen sits at the convergence of the Ruhr and the Rhine. The Rhine and Danube form Europe's

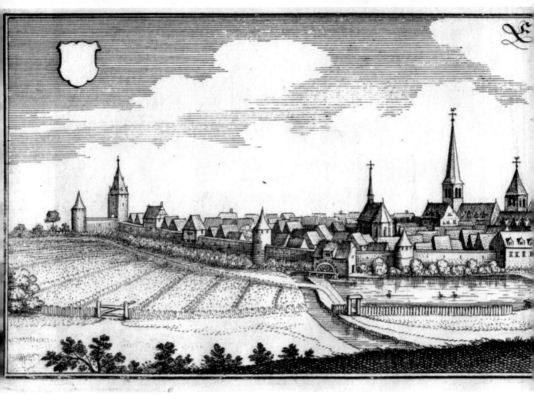

main water corridor, with the sources of both rivers almost meeting close to Germany's Freiburg.

For my grandmother, coming from Slovenia to the Ruhr Valley must have felt like going from farm to inferno. Those who lived up in the folds of Slovenia's lush green hills could sustain themselves by growing their own livestock, food and wine. On the other hand the Ruhr Valley, while once green and fertile, had turned into a wasteland.

At the time Gram and Grampa were in Essen, new coal mining operations were exploding in size and number. Mining camps were breeding grounds for constant, lethal, physical dangers; labor conditions were abysmal and pollution devastating. My grandfather later died of black lung disease.

I think that Grampa had served in the Austro-Hungarian military. Gram was tight-lipped about their past, but she did

Essen-Kupferstich-Merian

mention once that my grandfather had been in uniform. In those days people went to great lengths to avoid military service that could force them to fight their own kin.

At the dawning of the 20th century, scouts for the empire were combing the lands of eastern Europe, searching for young men to battle pretend enemies. Families did wherever they could to hide their young - behind the bookcase, under the chapel, in the tunnels, in mountain huts, in faraway farmsteads, under the floor boards. When Gram made her hasty departure from Essen, she and Grampa had already started a family, so they had daughters and a son to keep safe.

Coal mines already had begun to proliferate in the Essen area in the 16th century. By the turn of the 20th century, Essen had turned into an industrial megaplex, not only for coal but for weaponry. Weapon production was something the Celts knew well because they were always defending against attackers.[25]

My grandparents' escape from Europe stretched across two empires that used young boys as cannon fodder. **Kaiser Wilhelm II** was head of the German Empire from 1888 to 1918. The Austro-Hungarian Empire imposed feudalism in Central Europe between 1867 and 1918, From 1848 until he died in 1916, Franz Joseph I of Austria collected a bagful of titles like Emperor of Austria and King of Hungary, as well as ruler of the other states in the Habsburg monarch. Austria-Hungary was led by Emperor Franz Joseph, known for his childlike treatment

Essen. Ruhr
Museum Collection

**Ruhr Museum
Collection sword**

of war. While he had never served in the army himself, he portrayed himself in full military regalia, and delighted in playing endless war games with real human lives. So here are two dictators with an iron grasp on Europe. And those empires did not end until 1918 when the Kaiser finally abdicated. *"The reign of Kaiser Wilhelm II as King of Prussia and Emperor of Germany from 1888 to 1918 saw the meteoric rise of Germany as an economic and military power"* translates to *"he subjugated local people and worked them to death."*[25A]

Archaeology shows that around 850 C.E. an abbey led by Abbess Gerswid preceeded the cathedral; then it became an Ottoman Abbey. Additions built under the tenure of abbesses Agana and Hathwig were an outer crypt, a westwork a narthex and an external chapel. Abbesses directed the abbey until 1826; after 1803 the abbey became a parish church.

Essen in Europe

Essen Abbess, Mathilde swearing an oath holding staff topped by Celtic cross

Therapanu. Esssen Abbess. Evangeliar-Matthäus

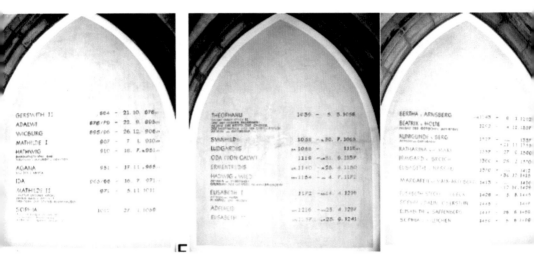

Essen. Lists of abbesses from 864 to 1826

Where does the abbey tradition of abbesses and mining intersect?

Homage to women - let's consider this specifically. Christianity's conversion of Europe meant that women no longer led the abbeys and thousands of women were burned at the stake under heresy laws.

At least 44 persons were burned to death during witch trials that took place in Essen in the 16th century, and they were predominantly women. Knowing how the Celts memorialized their heroes, we can only expect that every single one of the 60,000 women who died as witches under heresy laws have been memorialized. We can also expect that the image of each one of them was honored somewhere at some time. What we see now is only a small fraction of what has been destroyed – that we can deduce. "To great women, abbesses of the institution, who looked after and preserved the minster.

Essen Abbess, Mathilde swearing an oath holding staff topped by Celtic cross

ESSEN DOM
CLOISTER

So, Essen's central abbey was run by women for hundreds and hundreds of years up until the 19th century. The abbeys had presumably been a center for mining studies up until then. Why? Celts founded abbeys for further both education and production, and an abbey's offerings tended to be based on local resources and how to use them. It follows that mining expertise would be available near natural resources and repeatedly we have seen that this was the case.

Ruhr Valley from Volmarstein

What happened in the 19th century? Overlords exploited the coal in the area and imposed egregious living and working conditions on the people of Essen. This cannot have been an easy transition for Essen and it must have been vehemently opposed. Women were no doubt desperate to keep their men and boys from becoming human mules in the mines.

An important detail here is that coal was not widely used until the mid-19th century. That means that when my grandparents were in Essen, that area had been recently identified as a major target to exploit. That also means that until the mid-19th century, coal mining did not pollute the Ruhr Valley as it did in the lead-ups to the world wars. Why is this important? Because the scale and extent of the devastation that coal mining brought to the Ruhr Valley may have been a harbinger of what was to come, of the two world wars that look like thinly veiled excuses for destroying Europe.

Since the days my grandparents were in Essen, the area has gone an eye-popping transformation. UNESCO acquired the biggest coal mining operations and reconstructed a history of the mine that covers the time that my grandparents were there. I'd like to share some highlights of their reporting here.

Following is a pictorial account of Zollverein's mining activities in Essen in the 19th century as reported by UNESCO. It turns out, of course, that the area around Essen is rich with natural resources - and mining operations. I'd like to share with you here some of UNESCO's work that concerns the time when my grandparents lived in Essen, in the years before the 20th century dawned. In those years the coal industry was riveted on production and apparently unconcerned with the human tolls that related to its goals. It is possible that they worked for the Zollverein:

> Between 1880 and 1901 Zollverein was the most productive coal mine in the Ruhr District. From 1890, one million tons of pure hard coal were extracted per year. In 1900, more than 5000 miners worked at the Zollverein Coal Mine.

Here is an excerpted version of the account given by UNESCO at artsandculture.google.com/story/a-journey-into-historyzollverein/IgWxv2rmWYesrQ?hl=en

A JOURNEY INTO HISTORY

FROM INDUSTRIAL REVOLUTION TO UNESCO WORLD HERITAGE

By UNESCO World Heritage Zollverein

1847 –

First mine shaft sunk in Essen area; the new Cologne-Minden railway line was also an important advantage of the location

1856 –

First housing built for miners

1880 – 1901

Zollverein was the most productive coal mine in the Ruhr District. From 1890, one million tons of pure hard coal were extracted per year. In 1900, more than 5000 miners worked at the Zollverein Coal Mine

1880'S –

The by-products tar, ammonia, benzene and sulphuric acid were also extracted in addition to the coke, fuel and reductant for iron and steel production

1914 – 1918

World War I began and 27% of all men employed in the Ruhr mining industry were drafted for military service. There was a shortage of labor in the Ruhr coal mining industry

1939 – 1945[26]

More than 2500 of Essen's Jews were killed by Nazis

1991 –

UNESCO Heritage site awarded and central workshop converted into concert hall

Essen housing built in 1856

Zollverein women workers. Women, young people, older miners and forced labor were deployed at the coal mines and coking plants during the war

Essen mining "tenants" in 1860

Essen settlement houses

As I began to delve into my grandparents' history, it became clear that I needed to go back to Essen. I knew it had fallen to the depths of degradation because I had been there in the 1960's and could barely breathe the air.

We steeled ourselves for the worst. I had expected the grimy, smoggy, noisy, endlessly industrial place that I remembered from when I visited there 50 years ago. What a surprise to see what an enormous amount of work has been done to clean the whole valley! Now it is possible to see more of how it used to be before the Industrial Revolution, before the massive 19th century coal operations wreaked havoc with the Ruhr lands.

Beyond the abbeys that had been led by women for hundreds of years, we also found many tributes to women that seemed to acknowledge their work, especially in design and building. We found a Jewish cemetery with names that recalled Burgundians like Siegfried – and gravestones with Celtic-style designs. We found an old fortress with Burgundian-looking shutters. We found an old couple running a lovely villa on the mountaintop overlooking the valley where the locals still gathered.

We found very heavily fortified towns and villages.

We found women. Beautiful, lauded, remembered women.

THE RUHR VALLEY REMEMBERS
ITS WOMEN

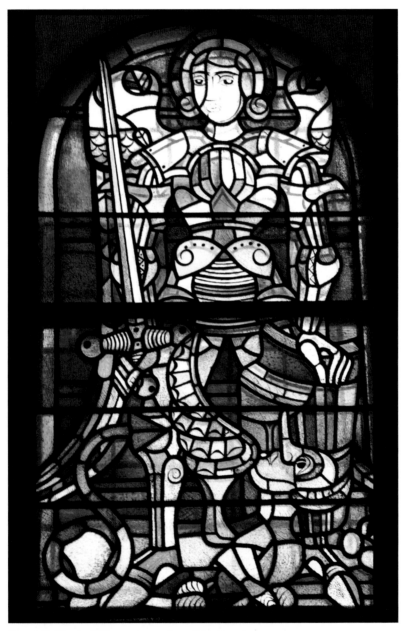

Essen Cathedral. Woman warrior with sword

Dortmund city hall – Has the head on this statue been replaced?

Dortmund. Statue of woman paid homage relating to a ship and fest hall

Lüdinghausen abbey. Note the crowned head underfoot, the sword & quill

Essen Dom. Women in white & gold

DIVÆ BARBARÆ SACR

Munster, likely former fest hall

DIVÆ APOLLONIÆ SACRŪ

Munster

Essen. Couple on either side of building entryway

Essen Saarn Abbey, details

Even now, though, these images carry the consequences of the Christian conquest. They are claimed by Christianity when there seems so little question that they are really Celtic heroes. Ironically, that may be the only way anything relating to the Celts still exists.

Burg Vischering Lüdinghausen, mill view.
Photo by Sebastian Meyer

Burg Vischering

Fortifications in the Ruhr Valley
from centuries and centuries past
stand like muffled cries for help,
bearing silent witness to the endless threats
this area has faced.

Within the next few years, the Knez family ended up in West Frankfurt, Illinois, another coal-rich region.

Gram & Grampa Knese in Essen

The death-trap conditions of the mines and the panoply of tributes to women in the former abbey may give us a hint of what Gram faced when she was escaping from Essen at around the turn of the 20th century. Gram left Europe from Essen - pregnant and with 3 children in tow - crossed Canada and then made it as far south as Oklahoma. My grandfather joined her there - that's where my mother was born. Gram gave birth to 16 children in all, including 3 sets of twins. Half died in childbirth or infancy.

Essen Dom from cloisters

OLD WORLD WAYS THAT SUSTAINED IMMIGRANTS IN NEW WORLD MISERIES

*Holding Close
the Reminders of Home*

Dobovica

THE DISPLACERS &
THE DISPLACED

Who are the Displacers?
Dictators wreak terror and fears.
The recent invasion of Ukraine
Gives a view of 2000 years.

What do troops do to women?
Those who stay are raped, brutalized
The ones who leave with their families -
They're Displaced - the emigrant "spies."

But within one generation
Their kids speak as well as home-landers.
They can recover quickly;
Schools can give a fresh start.

If we step into the future
Generally, what do we see?
Where are all the displacers
And where are those they've displaced?

In free states as a tourist,
You can travel freely around;
But in the lands of dictators,
You stay in your own compound.

he story of coal is fire after fire, explosion after explosion.[27]

Today's status of miners is abysmal.
Is this the way it's always been?

All of my grandparents fled their native land for the unknown shores of America. Eventually, they all ended up in the coal mines of southern Illinois. There - even now in the everything's-up-to-date-2000s - dread and death still hang like specters over the toxic pits that awaited them.

Kosolec on the way to Dobovica

Remarkably, all four came from villages within a 10-mile radius in Slovenia as the crow flies. But in that Sava River Valley filled with hollows, glens and twists, the only way to cut across is to fly. My two sets of grandparents didn't come to know each other until their children met and married in Chicago, many years later.

When my grandparents arrived, the mines in West Frankfort and Livingston had just started up. West Frankfort mine had opened in 1904; Livingston in 1902. Coal was relatively new to mining; wood had been used for cooking and heating up until the mid-19th century.

The name of the small town in Illinois that my maternal grandparents called home in the new world is called the old world name, West Frankfort. Here's what we know now.

- The West Frankfort mine went from zero production to the biggest producer in the state from 1900-1917
- Black lung increased in the 1900s because of the dust generated by new mining machinery
- 153 people died in 3 mine explosions, 1929-1951
- The annual wage of a miner in 1920 at the Livingston mine was $1,830.00, but by 1938 that wage fell to $250.00

The lives of my paternal grandparents seemed to follow a similar trajectory as my maternal ones. My paternal grandparents landed in the tiny town of Livingston, Illinois, a place that Wikipedia calls a village with about 763 people by today's reckoning, and a short 37 miles from St. Louis by interstate highway.

Here's an excerpted account of the mine:

In the fall of 1911, Livingston broke a record with an average of 4,029 tons per eight-hour day for 13 days. On September 29th, 4,264.90 tons were hoisted that amounted to 1,492 hoists per day or one hoist every 186 seconds. It took one hundred five railroad cars to hold this amount.

On March 1, 1912, Livingston again broke a record with 4,393 tons in seven hours and fifty minutes. The "Big Four" railroad gang of 75 men arrived in Livingston to extend the mine tracks to make facilities for getting out more coal. At first the coal was mined by hand and mules were used in the mine to pull the cars of coal. At one time there were forty mules in this mine. The

Livingston, Illinois, New Staunton Coal Company

mules were brought out of the mine only if the mine was to be idle for quite some time mainly in the summertime.

By 1937, things were so bad that miners had to get food from relief rolls, a federal government sponsored program, even while working. Others worked on WPA which was also a government program. Many of the youth participated in CCC camps that built state parks such as Pere Marquette Park. On December 22, 1954, about two in the morning, fire completely destroyed the hoisting tipple at the Livingston-Mt. Olive Coal Company Mine.[28]

> Men were springing forth, a black avenging army, germinating slowly in the furrows, growing towards the harvests of the next century, and their germination would soon overturn the earth. **Germinal**, by Emile Zola.

The book written by Emile Zola in 1885 encapsulates the dismal, desperate trap of the coal mines, as rich overlords pounded their men, mules and horses deep into the earth, straining to move tons of coal along endless steel rails, while their masters pumped more and more coal dust particles into the thick, dark air of cylindrical pathways to doom. More hours, more dust, work faster, earn less, while the coal overlords sat in their plush chambers, miles away from the grim, dirt and despair of their moles and slaves. Like the horses, the mules and men in the Livingston mines, were lowered into the depths when they were little, soon lost their health and eyesight as their lungs became laden with coal dust and their eyes could no longer penetrate the deep gloom. The men may have been luckier than the mules because they could come up into air that was slightly less toxic, slightly easier to breathe, and could for brief moments squint at those they loved in the worlds above. The mules never would be allowed to breathe air that was not compressed in the tunnels again and they would never see the faint light of day again. They would know the dank murk of subterranean labyrinths on an accelerated downhill plunge to their death, where they and their memory would be kept far away from the probing public eye.

Given the atrocious mining conditions in southern Illinois in the first half of the 20th century, it's not hard to see why my paternal grandparents worked with labor-activist Mother Jones to set up a labor union to stand up for miners' rights.[29] The fact that both sides of the family sent their children away at 12 years of age speaks unequivocally about how dire conditions must have been.

Besides the ever-present dangers of the mine's chambers, what was life like in the mining camps? Mining camps from that early 20th century era are often portrayed as men-only, but that does not seem to fit either my maternal or paternal grandparents' situations. Both sets of grandparents ran establishments where they served food and drink. My paternal grandparents ran a

Author's grandparents. Photo from the Mother Jones archives

tavern and my maternal grandparents operated a boarding house. All grandparents took part in gardening and food preparation. Mom's mother became the family's mainstay during her husband's illness and death.

What other specifics do I know about my grandparents' lives in the mining camps? I know that many nationalities met up in the mining towns because they used to come and visit us in Indiana. I also have a growing recognition of the pain suffered by our grandparents having to send their children away from the mining camp at an early age, a trauma for the entire family that never lessened.

When my mother was just 12 years old, she left West Frankfort to work in Chicago, lived with her older sister there and worked as household help. She married my father at age 16 and gave birth to my oldest sister at age 18. Soon after that, my parents moved out of the city to a new town in neighboring Indiana.

When her youngest children had left West Frankfort, my grandmother moved into their Indiana home with my parents. She lived with them for the next 40 years.

I don't know how she managed to do it, but Gram carried her baking pans along with her across Canada, to Oklahoma, to southern Illinois. Then she brought them to Indiana where they continued to be in daily use.

The attachment Gram had to them was palpable, to the point that I now count iron cookware along with other ancient milestones in human achievements. That must be why advances in cooking technology excite everyone – and it always must have been so.

Litija. Charcoal-making

Here, let me just say a word about the relative recency of coal mining, though. Heating used to be done with wood in the stove, not with coal in the furnace. Coal was not mined broadly until about the middle of the 19th century. Charcoal is another story.

Charcoal starts with wood, and has been in demand since the iron-smelting process was devised in pre-Christian times. You can still see little charcoal-makers dotting the Slovenian hills along the charcoal route in hills east of Ljubljana.

My grandparents' path seems to track mining's dehumanization. They came from bright forested hills to hard, barren depths with toxic air so thick that light could no longer penetrate. The situation only worsened in the new world where

A FARM
NEAR LITIJA

the coal mining craze drove insatiable lust for ever greater production.

In the mining camp in West Frankfort, in those dark times of my grandfather's illness and death, how did my grandmother hold the family together? How did she raise children who would pay homage to her at the lake? I can answer this with assurance because I used to stand in line for her perfect, puffy Krofi, hot from the stove, glistening with cinnamon and sugar.

The kitchen retains its luster for our family, and I am deeply grateful for that. I can think of no greater tribute to our forebearers for their heroic feats than food.

All four of my grandparents were passionate for the growing, harvesting and preparing of good food and drink, but particularly the enjoyment of it together. For this rich legacy they have left us, I would like to honor them with a small gallery of dining heritage.

Photo by Julia Stewart Lowndes

For The Love of Food!

Sundaes in the Port of Roses

Palacinka in Triglav National Park

Gibanica ingredients

Kremsnita

Gibanica

Potica

Strudelj

Blueberry cake at Otočec

Gram's blue pan

Sausage platter

Filled peppers

Chicken noodle soup

Knoedels

Herbs and spices at Ljubljana's market

Dobovica ovens

Fish from the pond

Vauclair Abbey medicinal plants

Breaded chicken

Seafood platter

Pears

Great times in Graz

Karst vineyards

TWELVE CURRENT TRIBUTES
TO THE OLD CULTURE
THAT WOULD HEARTEN
OUR ANCESTORS

Healing the Lands

Braunschweigische Zeche

Abbauzeit:	um 1530 bis 1772 mit Unterbrechungen
Erzmineralien:	Schwefelkies Kupferkies
	Magnetkies Malachit und Azurit in geringen Mengen
Gangarten:	Quarz, Kalkspat, Flußspat

Jewels of freedom's legacy –
the women, the Jews, the miners, the lands -
Just look how the conquerors treat them.

Let's retrieve ancestral balance
And respect the natural world.

Kudos to the EU and UN for righting longstanding wrongs.

mple proof shows that conquerors plunder the environment. Even worse, they don't remedy the damage they cause. Regardless of who caused the damage, though, nature needs to thrive in order to sustain healthy people and lands.

In this chapter I would like to look at some success stories in repairing the land from mining abuses. My book on Paris parks opened those worlds to me when I saw how some of Paris' most exquisite parklands were covering former quarries.[30]

Historians say that lands in the public domain used to be open to all for gathering food as well as quarrying stone. It seems all of a piece, then, that the public quarries on public lands should be rehabilitated as space for all to enjoy in common.

Here's what I have learned about mining, and it has come about in much the same way as my perceptions on refuge castles. Here's why. If you live in a town with a castle, the castle is where everyone goes. When I studied in Germany, I tried to hate castles because they were associated with aristocratic oppression and inequality. I gravitated to them, though, because of their architecture and settings.

Especially the locals seem to treat castles as their most cherished place to walk, to gather, to attend events. When I studied in Ljubljana, a number of us celebrated the fall by picking up chestnuts from the allée of trees leading to the castle. My Slovenian cousins were all married in their nearby castle, Wagensberg - now Bogensperk.

I went to an exhibit on witches with them in that castle and we then sat at the café overlooking the valley. It was particularly poignant because the exquisite 17th century book, "The Glories of the Duchy of Carniola" by Johann Valvasor31 originally was printed in that castle. Not only that, but the Duchess of Mecklenburg who began excavating Celtic artifacts in the region also was associated with the castle.32

Although castles may have been overtaken by the nobility for a time, they started out as refuge castles. They were built as part of the public domain and it's only right that are now being returned to public use. It's easy to dismiss both mines and castles as imperial, but we throw away our biggest treasures when we do. The mines and castles – like the secular abbeys and hot springs – were mainstays of the Celtic world that added beauty, depth and meaning to everyone's life.

Here I want to give a bow to the European Union and to the United Nations. The hand of the EU is apparent in the preservation work that we see going on all over Europe, from the wine hotel Tierras de Cebreros to the fest hall-converted to-church-back-to-fest-hall in the Hartz Mountains.

Spanish vineyards

Both the Sierra de Gredos and the Hartz mountains lie within areas that have been heavily mined. Both areas are rich with natural resources, have been badly scarred, but are being restored to their former luster.

Likewise, UNESCO has helped preserve ancestral caves and tunnels like Škocjan in Slovenia's Karst as well as mercury mines in Almaden and Idrija, now in Spain and Slovenia.

Restorations such as these are shaping an enlightened tourism that feels more like the old network of abbeys that offered learning and participation opportunities all across Europe.

So, let's consider Slovenia. As I set to work on this final chapter about restoration, I found a website for a mine in Litija – within 20 miles of where all my grandparents were born (as the crow flies).

1. MINES ARE TURNING INTO MUSEUMS

Here's where our inquiry hits paydirt.

The mine in Litija is reputed to be at one of the oldest and richest mineral deposits in the world. Twenty different kinds of minerals have been mined. Several smaller mines are still in operation and with similar mineralization, also in the vicinity of Litija.

These mines date back at least to the Iron Age, with minerals like galena or lead ore, sphalerite, cinnabar, chalcopyrite

Sava

and baryte numbering among the most important ones that are still mined even today.

The mine in Litija called Sitarjevec is now open to the public. www.mindat.org/loc-208676.html

According to their website:

The Sitarjevec Litija mine is a modern underground museum, that offers its visitors an insight into the diversity of the geological natural heritage, the world of bats, spiders and fungi, into the richness of the mining tradition and the interpretation of its richness through the eyes of artists.[33]

Škocjan caves exit. Photo TripAdvisor.com

2. CAVES ARE OPEN TO VISITORS

And it's not only Litija. Litija is in the center of the country. To the west lies Slovenia's karst region, a magical area with caves full of galleries, chambers and disappearing lakes. The karst landscape is said to be the most widespread landscape type in Slovenia, extending from the Ljubljana Marsh (Ljubljansko barje) to the Bay of Trieste.

According to UNESCO, *the karst region of Slovenia is among the richest areas in Europe in terms of flora and fauna and one of the global "hotspots" of biodiversity. There are some typical archaeological deposits of plant and animal species; this was where the first troglobitic cave-dwelling animal species were discovered and scientifically described.* whc.unesco.org/en/tentativelists/6072/

Slovenia's mineral composition is described by geologists as "colorful," and reaches back some 600 million years into the Precambrian era, apparently carving some 8,000 caves. The karst accounts for about a quarter of the entire country. Limestone is said to have been mined in the karst at least since the Iron Age, but has been mined for personal use far longer.

Cross Cave claims *to be the only naturally preserved tourist cave in Slovenia. The fragility of the caves presents the main obstacle for visitors, which prevents mass tourism and causes a restriction to the daily number of tourists, who can visit the water part of the cave, which is limited to four people.* krizna-jama.si/en/the-specifics-of-the-cave/#naturally-preserved

3. HOT SPRINGS RESORTS ARE RESUSCITATED

What heritage do the hot springs health resorts hold? Splits in geologic plates have been yielding hot water springs for millions of years. It is safe to assume that local habitants would have enjoyed that natural wonder, especially in winter.

In Alhama de Aragon, vestiges of the elegance and grace of the old spa town are virtually intact. The surrounding mountains, though, have been wracked by furious mining activity and a railroad has sliced through the heart of the town. Now, to reach the lake, gardens and lodge that you can see right next door, you walk around the whole periphery of the town. Now you enter the town on a one-way street because the railroad tunnel divides the main road. Now everyone knows when a train passes - it slashes its way through the heart of town with whistle at full-blast.

But the waters are still divine.[34]

Alhama, before railroad

Alhama de Aragon, after railroad

Alhama de Aragon

4. QUARRIES ARE TRANSFORMED INTO CITY PARKS

Buttes du Chaumont from manuscript Promenades de Paris

Promenades de Paris Buttes du Chaumont lakeside

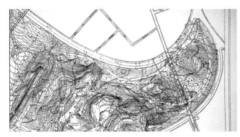

Buttes-Chaumont Plan

Promenades de Paris Buttes de Chaumont

Buttes de Chaumont, former gypsum, limestone quarry

Doué-la-Fontaine niche in cave

5. THE MEASURES OUR ANCESTORS TOOK TO SURVIVE ARE BECOMING CLEARER

Safehouses, hidden rooms within houses accessed by bookcases that swivel, Anne Frank's secret annex – these kinds of hiding places shielded women, Jews and others who were actively hunted in times of imperial assault. Mines and tunnels have been a key part of the escape system, in large part because one can survive there with fairly constant temperatures.

BELOW GROUND

Provins subterranean arches

ABOVE GROUND

Provins tower, roseraie

BELOW GROUND

Reims, Veuve Clicquot cellar, former chalk mines

ABOVE GROUND

Reims. Clicquot house garden

RUHR
VALLEY

6. COAL MINES ARE METAMORPHIZING INTO SANCTUARIES

Now the city from where my Grandma Knese escaped has returned to livable. I remember visiting in this area as a student at Bonn University in 1967 and could barely breathe the air. The Essen Zollverein – which was an association of industrial German cities – is a UNESCO Heritage site. Is the reason for her hasty departure wrapped up in this ghastly ecological nightmare that had been Essen's fate in that era?

Although the mining of coal was relatively recent, the scale of the operation has been massively destructive environmentally.

While coal may have been mined for thousands of years, it was not until the 19th and 20th century Industrial Revolution that it began to be extracted massively. For 20 years between 1880 and 1901 the Zollverein mining complex was the most productive in the Ruhr District. At that juncture, fueling the newly-invented steam engine, heating buildings and generating electricity drove the enormous jump in coal production and consumption. Until then wood had been used for heating, and amassed on a small-scale basis by families as they needed it.

Zollverein former coal mining center

Essen Zollverein

Loos-en-Gohelle. Mining tailings

7. POLLUTED MINING TOWNS ARE BEING REVITALIZED WITH CULTURE & EDUCATION

The town now known as Loos en Gohelle has been ravaged relentlessly by coal-mining and war. Near Lille in a former coal mining town in the North of France, Loos-en-Gohelle exemplifies how to gain freedom from fossil fuel dependence while still serving the real needs of locals.

Formerly Loos was one of the largest coal production centers in the Nord-Pas-de-Calais mining basin. The impact of coal mining on the environment has been onerous, with water and land polluted for decades. It became a shrinking city due to factory closures, job losses, social distress, mass unemployment, poverty, disenfranchised districts, land and water pollution, depletion of public resources, population loss.

In the 30 years since Loos has closed its mines, though, Loos has become a testing ground for energy transition policies, with solar panels now installed even on the remaining spoil tips. The Loos approach prioritizes local development. One of the first steps was to set up an energy renovation plan. In one section of town, houses have been completely renovated in accordance with new energy standards, insulated and equipped with solar panels and solar water heating.[36]

Tierras de Cebreros vineyards

Mountains near Idrija

8. THE EUROPEAN UNION IS HELPING TO RECONVERT DEFUNCT HALLS & VINEYARDS TO SECULAR USE

Grapes seem to grow where little else can. The stunning landscapes an hour west of Madrid are showcasing success stories of vineyard-clad hills graced by wine hotels.

Mines and wines have held ties at least since pre-Christian days and, potentially, much further into the past. Traces of wine in amphora have been found in various Celtic excavations, especially in what is now France and Germany. Châtillon-sur-Seine stands out with a funerary krater with traces of wine and the small figure of a woman sitting on the top rim. In pre-Christian times, amphora shards were so plentiful in Bibracte that they were used as construction fill.

The rugged Hartz mountains have been long maligned as infested with witches. Now restorations of charming old buildings are reinvigorating the hills and vales. From old thermal health resorts to railway stations to fest halls, archaeologists are uncovering gems that have been buried under mountains of falsehoods and rubble.

Wernigerode. Liebfraukirche is returning to secular use as a concert hall

9. UNESCO HERITAGE SITES ARE SAFEGUARDING ANCESTRAL MONUMENTS

In the western karst region, the old mercury mines of Idrija are now open to the public. The mining town here includes a castle, miners' living quarters, and a miners' theatre. Mercury mines at Almadén and Idrija have been UNESCO World Heritage Sites since 2012.

As with Bruges in Belgium, lace-making and mining go hand-in-hand in Idrija, and I want to talk a little bit more about that here. There appears to have been substantial communication among and within the various kinds of mining in Europe, and Idrija is a good example of that. Idrija is very tucked away, even by Slovenian measure. It's far off any of the main roads, and yet here you find one of the best tech museums in Europe.

The strong network associated with mining has been severed much in the way telephone lines used to be slashed by incoming invaders in more modern times. My grandparents story exemplifies the concerted attack on mining in the way that replacing women's heads with men's on statues serves as an icon of the women's story.

Here, in remote Idrija lies a Celtic microcosm, where natural beauty and bounty meld with architecture, mining and aesthetics. That's the way I see it.

Bohinj stream

Tršič nearby mountains, Slovenian side of Ljubelj

10. PARKLANDS ARE HELPING TO CONSERVE A FACTUAL HISTORICAL RECORD

The alpine northwest corner of Slovenia is rich with minerals, caves and tunnels, and wonderfully has been preserved by the Triglav National Park. Titles such as this say it all: Glow of Iron in the Bohinj Alpine Valley Iron Age Metallurgy in Slovenia. www.academia.edu/36297958/ Stara Fužina, which means old forges, seems to showcase the old mining ways in its charming structures and gardens.

The Iron Route in these mountains is an international project which brings together Alpine countries with a common past of mining, to reassess old mining sites and raise awareness of local and regional identities derived from 2500 years of mining tradition. New archaeological sites and forgotten iron ore mines in the eastern Alps have been discovered, documented and researched, resulting in a network of five high-altitude cultural and trekking trails called The Iron Route.

11. MISCREANTS AGAINST HUMANITY & NATURE ARE EXPOSED

The earth still shows scars 1500 years after Roman imperial travesties. Research has found that the Romans polluted European air for roughly 500 years, from around 350 B.C.E. to 175 CE. The lead mined by the Roman Empire in many areas of Europe polluted air at levels that declined once Rome fell and were not seen again until the Industrial Revolution. phys.org/news/2019-05-roman-polluted-european-air-heavily.html

UNESCO has gathered information regarding a mine in Spain called Médulas.

> In the 1st century AD, the Roman Imperial authorities began to exploit the gold deposits of this region, using a technique based on hydraulic power. After two centuries of working the deposits, the Romans left a devastated landscape. The traces are visible everywhere as sheer faces in the mountainsides and vast areas of tailings.

> The mining process, known to Pliny as ruina montium, made use of the immense power of large bodies of water. Water from springs, rain and melting snow was collected in large reservoirs, connected to the mines by a system of gravity canals over long distances. Excerpted.

Las Médulas mountains in Spain. A UNESCO renewal project
whc.unesco.org/en/list/803/

12. MINING MEMORIALS LINK LAYERS OF THE PAST

Not to be confused with Vršič, Tršič is a district at the far north of Slovenia right at the Austrian border. Here is what Mindat says about this former mercury mine:

A postcard from 1899 shows mined areas, in an apparent attempt to normalize the empire's massive mining destruction to the mountains.

On a somber but crucial note, the nearby Ljubelj pass was the only site of a Nazi labor camp in Slovenia. The camp was demolished in order to hide its existence, but an arena has been constructed there with a plaque that reads "J'accuse."

A website is dedicated to the memorial: www.mauthausenmemorial.org/en/Loibl/The-Concentration-Camp-Loibl

Tržič mercury mining area, in 1899

SPANISH
GOLD

CONCLUSION

The Hidden Women series begins and ends with gold. Gold adorns Europe's heroes - the men and women who defend liberty, the Franks and Burgundians who helped free Europe from the Roman Empire, Charlemagne's family of abbey-founders, martyrs of the Christian conquest and the Michelsberg mining culture that extracts the earth's treasures with care and respect for the benefit of the common good.

Here are the essential elements.

1. Before the Christian era, Celts had a common culture across Europe of mining, technology, communication, art, science, law, astronomy, trade. Women had an equal place with men in a free and open society

2. When the Roman Empire invaded and occupied Europe's Celtic lands that extended from Britain to Hungary and beyond, they instituted the subjugation and human-trafficking of women as men's property. They also abused the earth in their feverish attempts to extract its treasures. Later empires followed their lead

3. Those ideas continue to dominate today. The Christian conquest attempts to erase the women's role from the annals of history, even to the point of replacing

the heads on female statues with male ones. The Church wrongly identifies as Christian martyrs the very women that the Church itself burned at the stake as witches. Today the Christian church still attempts to claim women's bodies as men's vessels - to control, restrict and sacrifice at themale supremacists' whim

These feudal attitudes wreck families, weaken culture and wreak havoc on the environment. Breaking free of Christianity's subjugation requires acknowledgement that the Christian Church acts as a male supremacist dictatorship that harms women. Those claiming to be Christian must own the horrors of Christianity - a father offering his son as a human sacrifice and the Schadenfreude notion of an eternal fiery afterlife for non-Christians.

No tax benefits or subsidies should be available to any organization that targets and harms women, including Christian organizations. Education should be made free and open to all, regardless of gender. Religious officials must be held accountable for their discriminatory acts against women, children, minorities and the common good.

Dancing Men & Women of the Vineyard,

Monthermé · · · · · Donzenac · · · · · Pavia

Celebration – not contrition – that's the overarching
theme of these memorials to women that were converted into
Christian martyrs. Just look at the sway and grace of their
stances. The movement in the statues carries the same festivity
of the figurines of men from the Iron Age, also shown here.
Even despite the arrows and flames later added by the Christian
conquerors, the homage to these women shines through.

May the world regain its lost
freedoms and shared prosperity

Mines, Castles, Fest Halls & Abbeys

Judenburg   Essen   Donzenac

Iron Age figurines of men dancing

ENDNOTES

I FEMALE MINE WORKERS IN THE MIDDLE AGES

Although women and girls probably worked in mining since antiquity, the earliest known written references to female manual labourers in mining are in the 13th and 14th century records of the royal lead and silver mines at Bere Alston, on the border between Devon and Cornwall. The mines were bordered on three sides by a loop of the River Tamar, the east bank of which has been the traditional boundary between Devon and Cornwall since 936. The mines themselves were on the Devon side of the border at Bere Alston itself, but the surface-level smelters were on the Cornish side at Calstock as there was a readier supply of timber for use in the furnaces.

Although the mining itself was carried out by men, female workers were employed to sort ore for crushing, to prepare the bone ash used as a flux during the smelting process, and for general manual labour. An adult woman was paid up to one penny per day, and young girls between 1/2 and 2/3 of a penny. Miners and other skilled labourers at Bere Alston were recruited from throughout England and Wales, and from the evidence of surnames in the records it appears that many of the female labourers were the wives and daughters of these incomers rather than locally recruited women.

The area's population collapsed both during and after the Black Death. Those miners who had survived the pandemic left mining to work in farming, in which wages had doubled owing to the severe labour shortage, and the mines of Bere Alston were abandoned.

Although women and girls were almost certainly employed at the lead and silver mine at Bere Alston, and also a few records have so far been of female workers at tin works on Bodmin Moor and around Redruth and Marazion in the 14th century.

2. Here's a 4500-year-old temple at a river source in India: www.facebook.com/panchganilover/videos/ krishnabaitemple-is-supposed-to-be-source-of-the-krishna- river-the-temple-was-b/715323553096106/#

ii. en.wikipedia.org/wiki/Temple

iii. whc.unesco.org/en/list/1006/#:~:text=The%20Neolithic%20 flint%20mines%20at,settlement%20of%20the%20same%20 period

5. Researchgate. www.researchgate.ne https://whc.unesco.5 org/en/list/1006/#:~:text=Neolithic%20populations%20 could%20thus%20pass,props%20and%20lowering%20of%20 the

7 *Stollen* means [mining] gallery and Berg translates to hill. There are two Stolbergs in the Eifel & Harz mountains. Stolberg in the Harz Mountains & at the fringes of the Eifel mountains date at least back to the 700's. Iron, copper, silver, tin and gold were extracted from the Harz Mountain Stolberg. The Stolberg near Aachen in the Eifel mountains also shows lots of slate.

Both Stolbergs are known for mining. The Stolberg in the Eifel Mountains is in the Eschweiler District and at the Stolberg in the Harz Mountains is a memorial to concentration camp prisoners murdered there.

8 www.salzwelten.at/en/blog/salzburg-saltmine

10 orau.org/health-physics-museum/articles/jachymov-cradle-of-the-atomic-age.html

11 en.wikipedia.org/wiki/Rammelsberg

12 The mural uncovered in a Regensburg hall also shows a reptile at the foot of a triumphant woman raising a goblet after perhaps vanquishing a foe.

13 www.alaturka.info/en/history/antiquity/3971-noricum-a-celtic-kingdom-in-today-s-austria 14 en.wikipedia.org/wiki/Noric_

14 en.wikipedia.org/wiki/Noric_steel

15 **AQUILEIA**

Two thousand years ago, Aquileia on the Adriatic coast of north-east Italy was one of the biggest cities of the world. Before the Roman invasion, *Celtic* people lived here and called it Akylis. At that time it was an important centre for the trade of amber. kyabaat.blogspot.com › roman-port-of-aquilea

Jewish artisans established a flourishing trade in glass-work. Metal from Noricum was forged and exported. The ancient Venetic trade in amber from the Baltic continued. Wine, especially its famous Pucinum was exported. Olive oil was imported from Proconsular Africa. By sea, the port of Aquae Gradatae (modern Grado, Friuli-Venezia Giulia) was developed. On land, Aquileia was the starting-point of several important roads leading outside Italy to the north-eastern portion of the empire — the road (Via Julia Augusta) by Iulium Carnicum (Zuglio) to Veldidena (mod. Wilten, near Innsbruck), from which branched off the road into Noricum, leading by Virunum (Klagenfurt) to Laurieum (Lorch) on the Danube, the road leading via Emona into Pannonia and to Sirmium(Sremska Mitrovica), the road to Tarsatica (near Fiume, now Rijeka) and Siscia (Sisak), and the road to Tergeste (Trieste) and the Istrian coast. See en.wikipedia.org/wiki/Aquileia

16 MAGDALENA MINES IN THE NEW WORLD

In Mexican Magdalena, which lies in the Jalisco region fire opals are still widely mined. Yet another Magdalena lies even further south where the Andes mountains hide ancient gold. The Magdalena River Valley keeps its pre-conquistador, pre-Columbian secrets.

Three bits of interest about the New Mexican connection. One is that New Mexico has been inhabited by humans for the past 20,000+ years, according to recent archeological findings. Secondly, it is well known that massive displacements have taken place in Europe that caused people to set sail and flee to places like the Americas, often with captors in pursuit. Some Galls from France apparently came to Nova Scotia and then were forced to flee again, all the way to Louisiana, as recounted in Wordsworth's Evangeline.

Thirdly, the mining town of Magdalena in New Mexico prizes its public domain. Magdalena has a city hall, a Magdalena-hall hotel and parklands. In this remote mining town locals gather regularly at the library to study computer coding.

17 www.nature.com/articles/s41598-019-54222-x#citeas Published: 28 November 2019 Geochemistry of Gold Ores Mined During Celtic Times from the North-Western French Massif Central.

18 www.jstor.org/stable/526671

19 www.academia.edu/36297958/Glow_of_Iron_in_the_ Bohinj_Alpine_Valley_Iron_Age_Metallurgy_in_Slovenia

20 *Naturalis Historia, XXXIII*, 70, In year 74 C.E. describing the way Roman mined for gold in Spain.

21 Note also that the 16th century author's name is Georgius Agricola, described as a German Humanist scholar, mineralogist and metallurgist, son of Gregor Bauer, whose full name was Georg Pawer from Leipzig University. There are several fascinating aspects to this. "Agricola" is likely is the Celtic term for agriculture. The German translation of Agricola is "Bauer," but Bauer in German literally means builder. "Bauen" = to build. I strongly suspect that this reflects the Christian conquest of this area of Europe, because the "Bauer" were the builders that the Christian subjugated as appendages to the lands they overtook. In other words, Bauer has come to mean "serf" or slave in the German language, but the Celts were known to have possessed building skills far superior to those who conquered them. Thus, this tension in the translation of "Agricola" to "Bauer" is a sign of the cultural turmoil that ensued from the Christian takeover of people technological more advanced than they, and who also prized and celebrated their advancements, as is aptly

demonstrated in this book by Gregorius Agricola. Most strikingly and beautifully, this book demonstrates the techniques that developed in Europe over the millennia by those passionate about extracting the earth's treasures.

22 *De Re Metallica*, Georgius Agricola, Translated from the First Latin Edition of 1556 by Lou Henry and Herbert Hoover, with Biographical 22 Introduction, Annotations and Appendices upon the Development of Mining, Methods, Metallurgical Processes, Geology, Mineralogy & Mining Law from the. earliest times to the 16th century.

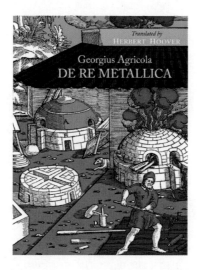

24 en.wikipedia.org/wiki/List_of_people_executed_for_witchcraft

25 Swords from Noricum were highly prized. Noricum lies partly in Carinthia — now split between Austria and Slovenia — and Noricum used to be famous for ore rich in manganese. The capital of Celtic Noricum was the gold mining town of Magdalensberg.

The Celts in Noricum discovered that their ore made superior steel around 500 B.C.E and had built a major steel industry, so Celtic weaponry manufacture was longstanding and well-known. The Romans obviously wanted both the gold and Noric swords, and eventually succeeded in overtaking Noricum. Unrelentingly, empires harnessed Celtic resources and skills to make the very weapons that empires used against Celts, and Noricum is a prime example of that.

26 In the Second World War the Krupp family from Essen apparently manufactured weapons for the Nazis, used 26 slave labor in its factories and ran a facility at Auschwitz concentration camp.

ESSEN'S ALTE SYNAGOGE THAT SURVIVED KRISTALLNACHT

Jewish Historical Society of Delaware

https://jhsdelaware.org›Blog

In front there is a stone memorial to the more than 2,500 of Essen's Jews exterminated by the Nazis from 1939 to 1945. 27 Coal mining's human tolls.

27 **COAL MINING'S HUMAN TOLLS**

If god ever existed, he died in the mines
The coal dust, the loads, the ear-splitting noise,
No one could last very long.

The plague of the coal mines arose as a way
For the rich to grow richer and richer and richer
Miners lives didn't matter.

On both sides of the sea, coal laid a trap;
Its barons pulled everyone in and
Exploded old joys of "berg" mining

28 Livingston had its start by the building of the railroad and the opening of a mine in the neighborhood. Livingston 28 was laid

out about 1904 by the heirs of John Livingston. About 1903 the Cleveland, Cincinnati, Chicago and St. Louis Railroad better known as the "Big Four" built a railroad from Hillsboro to East St. Louis passing through Madison County. It was in Olive Township along this rail line that a mine was sunk in September, 1904.

Beginning in 1904, the Deering Coal Mine Company took Franklin County and West Frankfort from no coal production in 1900 to being the #1 coal producer in Illinois by 1917. Once the mines opened, the population increased 3,500 in seven years. By 1927, West Frankfort's population had reached 19,896. Railroad tracks were laid 4 miles west of Frankfort to link with Chicago, Paducah, and Memphis.

- 1929 coal mine explosion that killed 7 people.
- 1947 coal mine explosion that killed 27 people.
- 1951 coal mine explosion that killed 119 men.

The machine shop was equipped with lathes, drill press and pipe machines which were necessary to every mine.

March 1914, brought about the hoisting of 103,694.6 tons of coal with only fifteen hours lost that month due to lack of cars and the funeral of a man killed in the mine. The mine was closed for ten days in January 1917 because the drivers wanted to work eight hours and be paid for nine. The company wouldn't grant that request so the miners voted to go back to work. A new coal crusher was installed with a capacity of five hundred tons per hour.

In April 1930, orders were received from St. Louis to close down the mine. The mine employed approximately 400 men of which 90% lived in Livingston.

The reason given for the shutdown was inability to secure sufficient business to warrant working the mine. After being without work during part of 1930 and all of 1931 in January, 1932, a group of ten Livingston businessmen formed a new company named Livingston-Mt. Olive Coal Company. www.angelfire.com/il/livingstonillinois/history/Book5.pdf

29 **Mary G. Harris Jones** (1837 (baptized) – November 30, 1930), known as **Mother Jones** from 1897 onwards, 29 was an Irish-born American labor organizer, former schoolteacher, and dressmaker who became a prominent union organizer, community organizer, and activist. She helped coordinate major strikes, secure bans on child labor, and co-founded the socialist trade union, the Industrial Workers of the World (IWW).

After Jones's husband and four children all died of yellow fever in 1867 and her dress shop was destroyed in the Great Chicago Fire of 1871, she became an organizer for the Knights of Labor and the United Mine Workers union. In 1902, she was called "the most dangerous woman in America" for her success in organizing miners and their families against the mine owners. [1] In 1903, to protest the lax enforcement of the child labor laws in the Pennsylvania mines and silk mills, she organized a children's march from Philadelphia to the home of President Theodore Roosevelt in New York.

30 Stewart, Jacqueline, *Parks and Gardens in Greater Paris*, Éditions Axel Menges, Fellbach, 2012.

31 Johann Weikhard von Valvasor, *The Glories of the Duchy of Carniola*, Nuremberg, edited by 31 Erasmus Finx, 1689.

32 Greis, Gloria Polizzotti, A Noble Pursuit: The Duchess of Mecklenburg Collection from Iron Age Slovenia (Peabody Museum Collections Series), Peabody Museum Press, 2006.

33 rudniksitarjevec.si/en A spoil tip (also called a boney pile, culm bank, gob pile, waste tip or bing) is a pile built of accumulated

spoil – waste material removed during mining. These waste materials are typically composed of shale, as well as smaller quantities of Carboniferous sandstone and other residues.

34 **WATER TEMPLE AT ALHAMA**

35 A spoil tip (also called a boney pile, culm bank, gob pile, waste tip or bing) is a pile built of accumulated spoil – waste material removed during mining. These waste materials are typically composed of shale, as well as smaller quantities of Carboniferous sandstone and other residues.

36 corpwatchers.eu/en/investigations/cities-versus-multinationals/loos-en-gohelle-from-coal-to-renewables-36 is-there-a-future-for-asmall-town

Essen Kupferdreh Hellersberg Steinkiste

APPENDIX

WHAT 250 OBERHAUSEN MIGHT MEAN

Early Essen's residents must have prized megalithic tombs as their earliest preserved architecture. In the Iron Age they carefully covered graves and mines, making them into tumuli and underground galleries. Townspeople must have watched with horror as imperial forces ripped through long-tended, hand-crafted mounts that had so carefully encased their ancestral and geologic treasures – all apparently in pillaging gold and other valuables.

Consider one grave in Essen that dates from 3000 B.C.E. and is above-ground. The megalithic tomb appears to lend support to a theory about why burial chambers came above ground.

Before the Iron Age, Celts apparently paid homage to their heroes by providing sizable underground chambers. Celts started burying their dead above-ground probably to safeguard grave treasures. This practice seems to have begun around the start of the Common Era. In Germany alone there are more than 250 places called Oberhausen, literally, "houses above."

It is still possible to find examples of stand-alone style houses in old cemeteries. Here it is important to remember that Celts named literally. "Hausen" that house the dead is in keeping with both the way Celts named and the way Celts memorialized their heroes.

Around the Essen area alone there are more than 34 places that end in "hausen." Here's an imcomplete list: Albringhausen, Bövinghausen, Brockhausen, Bruckhausen,

Brünninghausen, Buschhaus, Dahlhausen, Deininghausen, Dreihausen, Echthausen, Ellinghausen, Frohnhausen, Funckenhausen, Heiligenhaus, Heringhausen, Holsteinhausen, Holthaus, Hosterhausen, Kaldenhausen, Kurhausstrasse, Lüdinghausen, Menglinghausen, Nienhausen, Oberhausen, Oberdahlhausen, Kloster Oelinghausen, Recklinghausen, Renninghausen, Rheinhausen, Röhlinghausen, Schmehausen, Schwieringhausen, Vierhausen, Vöckinghauen, Westhusen (Dutch variation).

Recklinghausen. A fortified town that contains a Jewish cemetery

Veržej

Bugue cemetery. Blue door, white Haus

Cambrai. La Porte de Paris cemetery Hausen with outdoor seating

Caviglio. Row-Hausen

Hausen traditions from around Europe

I would suggest that the proliferation of "houses above" signals something significant, a change in burial practices. In the Iron Age, Celts built huge underground chambers - like full-size homes for the dead – and covered them with earth to make small hills called tumuli.

Once attackers like Julius Caesar invaded Europe and discovered tumuli during the century before the Common Era, though, he no doubt gave his soldiers plundering rights. They could keep what they could steal. J.C. gave his legions the right to capture natives and enslave them – and to seize their possessions, including their lands. The tumuli were rich in golden homages, because the Celts crafted exquisite golden jewelry to honor their heroes and they laid it in their graves.

How to guard against grave robberies? Make the graves smaller and put them closer? Instead of the vast underground burial chambers, build smaller replicas and cluster them together above ground. Call them "Hausen" since they house family memories of the past.

"Oberhausen"

Thus, "Hausen" may well have been the intermediate answer to grave-looting. Later, in response to above-ground tombs also being burglarized, the memorials likely were moved into heroes' halls. In the heroes' halls, gilded images of the deceased would be on display, whether or not the remains were buried there.

These may be "Oberhausen," or above-ground tombs, that are clustered around the double-towered fest hall between the moat and the walled city of Aachen. The valuables would not be placed in these replica-houses, but in the heroes hall that lies inside the protection of the walls.

Some Hausen are complete with roofs, stained glass windows, hearth and mantel, front steps and even chairs to accommodate visitors who come to place wreaths and tributes on the mantel. Examples shown here come from across Europe, but they likely illustrate longstanding customs that the term Oberhausen might represent.

Here's one more thought about the Hausen. What we sometimes see is that the name endures although the object of the naming no longer exists. Here's what I mean in two instances regarding abbeys. In the town of Judenburg a street is called "Rue de l'Abbaÿe" where no visible traces of the abbey remain. In the area of "Place de l'Abbaÿe" in Wiesbaden, it takes little imagination to see where the layout of the abbey might have been and what buildings might have been out-buildings for the abbey.

The same may hold true for Hausen. Places named "Hausen" may keep their name even though the original burial grounds with replica houses for the dead have been moved or destroyed. The Oberhausen near Essen, for example, has fifteen cemeteries, including a Jewish cemetery.

Let's think generally now of times when we know there were massive killings in Europe – the Roman Empire, the Crusades and the witch hunts. We'll set aside for a moment the wars of the 20th century. footnote Julius Caesar's mass killings occurred in the century before the Common Era; the Crusades from 10th to 13th centuries, the witch burnings from 14th to 18th centuries.

Caviglio. Row-Hausen

Starting with the Caesar's rampages around the beginning of the Common Era - occasionally it is possible to find early graves identified as Roman. Predictably, in Celje there is a Roman necropolis. Why? Celeia, the old Celtic name, literally means "Celtsville" and ends with a typical Celtic "ia" and the town itself exhibits many other Celtic qualities as well. Similarly, the museum in Lyon - Lugdun or Lugdunon in Gallic – features numerous grave steles from around the beginning of the Common Era. Celje, in my opinion, would have been the classic example of a Roman overtaking because Imperial Rome took the most thriving Celtic sites and falsely proclaimed everything about them to be Roman.

Further, I suggest that gravestones portraying family members together tend to be Celtic; those showing a sole military man are likely Roman, regardless of how they are labelled. Early examples of gravestones that are likely Celtic - showing bas reliefs of couples or families - can be found at museums that feature Celts, like those at Bourges, Lyon, Carcassonne, Stuttgart and Ljubljana.

MY FAMILY'S MOTHER JONES MEMORY

by John Weber
www.motherjonesmuseum.org

My Mom grew up in Chicago and is of Slovene and Lithuanian heritage. My Dad, of Swiss, Czech, and German heritage, also grew up downstate in Illinois. Through my great aunt, I learned how powerful the memories of immigrant struggles and of memories of Mother Jones can be.

My Mom and Dad met through our extended family who, on both sides, live in neighboring small coal mining towns (Staunton and Livingston) in downstate Illinois near Mt. Olive, where Mother Jones is buried.

My Great-Aunt Helen Straub (née Widmar) was born in 1921, the youngest of 8 siblings. She passed in 2017 at age 96. Aunt Helen told our family about the life of my Great-Grandfather John Andrew Widmar (1879-1959), an immigrant coal miner from the Zasavje region of Slovenia. Zasavje is a steep, hilly, rich and fertile region of subsistence farming. Coal (brown coal) was historically mined nearby in the Sava River valley at Trbovlje and Hrastnik. The men of John Widmar's time combined farming and coal mining to survive. Many of our living Slovene relatives still do subsistence farming, traveling down from the Zasavje villages and hills to bigger towns in the region and to the capital city of Ljubljana to work non-farming jobs, attend schools and university, etc.

It's likely that John Andrew Widmar, like many other men of his time and place in Austro- Hungarian central Europe, was recruited to come to the Pennsylvania anthracite coal area by a coal company agent of American coal company agent around 1900.

John Andrew Widmar came to Ellis Island, and then to Yukon, PA, USA circa 1905 to work in the western Pennsylvania bituminous coal fields. His wife, Josephine Marie Widmar (nee Povše), followed shortly afterward.

A powerful memory for my Aunt Helen was when her father took her to Mother Jones' funeral in 1930 at the Union Miners Cemetery, Mt. Olive, Illinois. Aunt Helen would have been 9 years old then. This event stuck with her well into her 90s, seeing the many people who made it one of the largest funerals in Illinois history. It must have been quite memorable! Many other immigrant miners and their families also attended the Mother Jones' funeral to show their love and respect for her and her work.

Aunt Helen's oldest brother, Jack (the second John Andrew) Widmar, who was born 1907 in Yukon, PA, worked with his Dad in the Livingston and Staunton, IL mines, probably starting at around age 10, before he moved to Chicago. Helen must certainly have heard first-hand about the working conditions in both the Pennsylvania and Illinois coal mines that Mother Jones fought to change. I believe this is why her attending the 1930 funeral was such a memorable event that she felt compelled to share.

Thanks to opportunities that my Slovene coal-mining ancestors helped to create, I am a Geology Professor at a state university in the Midwest. I take many of my classes on annual spring field trips to study the geology of Illinois and Missouri. One of the most impactful stops that we make on these geo-pilgrimages is the Mother Jones monument and Union Miner's Cemetery in Mt. Olive. Students are blown away that this seemingly mundane place has such a deep history, and that geology drives history and affects human lives and families in such a fundamental way.

THE LAST SHIPS FROM HAMBURG

by Steven Ujifusa

Between 1881 and 1914 10 million people crossed the Atlantic from Europe to America, over 2.5 million including my grandparents, Max & Dora Gottlieb.

This mass exodus was facilitated by three businessmen whose involvement in the Jewish-American narrative has been largely forgotten: Jacob Schiff, the managing partner of theinvestment bank Kuhn, Loeb & Company, who used his immense wealth to help Jews to leave Europe; Albert Ballin, managing director of the Hamburg-American Line, who created a transportation network of trains and steamships to carry them across continents and an ocean; and J. P. Morgan, mastermind of the International Mercantile Marine (I.M.M.) trust, who tried to monopolize the lucrative steamship business. Though their goals were often contradictory, together they made possible a migration that spared millions from persecution.

BIBLIOGRAPHY

Agricola, Georgius, *De Re Metallica*, translated from the First Latin Edition of 1556 by Lou Henry and Herbert Hoover, Dover Publications, Inc., New York, 1950.

Davis, Dan, *These Ancient Mines Transformed Prehistoric Europe*, Dan Davis History, www.youtube.com/watch?v=FL92iskCSZA

Greis, Gloria Polizzotti, *A Noble Pursuit: The Duchess of Mecklenburg Collection from Iron Age Slovenia* (Peabody Museum Collections Series), Peabody Museum Press, 2006.

Małachowski, K. (2018). The biggest surface mining disaster in Poland and its economic results. *European Journal of Service Management*, 4 (28/2), 247–255. DOI: 10.18276/ejsm.2018.28/2-31.

Mindat Mindat.org is the world's largest open database of minerals, rocks, meteorites and the localities they come from. Mindat.org is run by the not-for-profit Hudson Institute of Mineralogy.

Valvasor, Johann Weikhard von, *The Glory of the Duchy of Carniola*, 1689, encyclopedia published in Nuremberg in 1689 by the polymath Johann Weikhard von Valvasor. It is the most important work on his homeland, the Duchy of Carniola, the present-day central part of Slovenia. He is known as a pioneer in the study of karst topography. Together with his other writings, until the late 19th century his best-known work— the 1689 *Glory of the Duchy of Carniola*, published in 15 books in four volumes—was the main source for older Slovenian history, making him one of the precursors of modern Slovenian historiography, per Wikipedia.

Zola, Emile, *Germinal*, 1985, G. Charpentier, appeared first as a series as Les Rougon-Macquartin the periodical *Gil Blas*. A realistic account of a coalminers' strike in northern France that happened a century previously.

See generally

Cunliffe, Barry, *the Ancient Celts*, Oxford University Press, 2018, 2nd edition.

Green, Miranda J, *The Celtic World*, Routledge, New York, 1996.

Kruta, Venceslas, *Le monde des anciens Celtes*, Éditions Yoran, Fouesnant, 2015.

Special thanks to Wikipedia, Amazon, Google search engines and maps.

INDEX

HIDDEN WOMEN

A History of Europe
Celts & Freedom

by Jacqueline Widmar Stewart

HIDDEN WOMEN

Celtic Burgundy & Europe

by Jacqueline Widmar Stewart

HIDDEN WOMEN

Frankish Splendor & Valor
in Celtic Europe

by Jacqueline Widmar Stewart

HIDDEN WOMEN

Charlemagne's Celtic Domain

by Jacqueline Widmar Stewart

HIDDEN WOMEN

Legacies from a Free
Celtic Europe

by Jacqueline Widmar Stewart

HIDDEN WOMEN

Mines, Temples & Parklands
in Celtic Europe

by Jacqueline Widmar Stewart

HIDDEN WOMEN BOOKS SERIES OVERVIEW

In this multi-disciplinary study narrated by photography, poetry, maps and text, Hidden Women books bring vantage views into a wealthy, innovative, nature-loving Celtic civilization that spanned Europe from the British Isles to Hungary and beyond. Starting from archaeological finds and following right up to the present-day, the author traces some of the common threads that were beautifully woven by both genders over some 3000 years.

One discrepancy stands out: Europe's pre-Christian residents esteemed women, whereas invaders and imperialists do not. By embracing the Celtic legacy of freedom and equality, the world can regain an open, cosmopolitan society that honors achievement regardless of gender.